How to Stimulate the Child's Brain

What are executive functions and why are they important? How can they be developed effectively in children and adults? Many children, adolescents, and adults experience difficulties and disorders that stem from poor executive functioning, such as ADHD, dyslexia, or behavioral problems. Concentration, working memory, planning, and impulse control are executive functions of the brain that must be trained and put into practice in order to perform well and function effectively in different contexts (educational/work, emotional, and social).

This book brings together the concepts necessary to understand the basic functioning of the brain, as well as the relationship between its different parts.

- It describes the main executive functions, such as concentration, impulse control, emotional self-regulation, and processing speed, among others.
- It contains 100 exercises to stimulate the brain in a simple and fun way. Enhancing your executive functions is within your reach.

Take advantage of the opportunity this book offers you: achieve a satisfactory adaptation to your environment and those around you.

Rafa Guerrero is currently the Director of Darwin Psychologists and a Professor at the Faculty of Education of the Complutense University of Madrid (UCM). He also teaches at the Cardenal Cisneros University Center, University of Alcalá de Henares, and is a lecturer at the Rey Juan Carlos University (URJC). He is a member of the Spanish Society of Psychosomatic Medicine and Psychotherapy (SEMPP), a member of the Institute for the Development and Application of EMDR (IDAE), a regular contributor to the newspapers *El País* and the *Diario ABC*, a lecturer at national and international conferences, and a trainer of teachers and parents in numerous schools and educational centers in Spain.

How to Stimulate the Child's Brain

100 Exercises to Boost Concentration, Memory, and Other Executive Functions

Rafa Guerrero

Routledge
Taylor & Francis Group
NEW YORK AND LONDON

Designed cover image: Getty Images

First published in English 2027
by Routledge
605 Third Avenue, New York, NY 10158

and by Routledge
4 Park Square, Milton Park, Abingdon, Oxon, OX14 4RN

Routledge is an imprint of the Taylor & Francis Group, an informa business

Como estimular el cerebro del niño (2nd edition) by Rafa Guerrero

ISBN: 978-1-041-32871-1 (hbk)
ISBN: 978-1-041-28046-0 (pbk)
ISBN: 978-1-003-79433-2 (ebk)

DOI: 10.4324/9781003794332

Typeset in Times New Roman
by codeMantra

Page 124 - *The injury of Phineas Gage*, based on Ratiu (2004). Summary of Ratiu's analysis is available at John Darrell Van Horn (2012)

Access the Support Material: www.routledge.com/9781041280460

To all my patients, with whom we have had such a good time enhancing their executive functions.

Contents

Foreword

The knowledge of the structure and function of the brain provided by neuroscience is rapidly generating new data that is influencing many different fields of the humanities. These fields range from philosophy to ethics, aesthetics, economics, and, more recently, education. And, of course, this impact is being felt most notably in psychology and the study of behavior, which, in turn, are nourished by the knowledge provided by neuroscience itself. Clearly, this knowledge about the brain and its impact on the humanities transforms and changes the society in which we live, and these changes are ultimately responsible for the constant and successive evolution of cultures.

A practical consequence of all of the above is the extension of all this new knowledge to different areas of society and, of course, especially to the different disciplines or professional groups to which new books are dedicated, as is the case with this particular book on education and teaching. Such books are necessarily written (or should be) in accessible language, of course, but solidly based on knowledge of both neuroscience and the corresponding humanistic disciplines. This is the case with this book by Rafa Guerrero. It is written in a very didactic and accessible way and deals with one of the topics that perhaps has the greatest impact today in the world of neuroeducation, namely executive functions or, if you like, the topic of individuality and complex social functions.

The truth is that for thousands of years, human beings have struggled almost exclusively to stay alive in environments where biological survival was the supreme value. In contrast to this, in today's democratic social contexts, far removed from those times, humanity's struggle focuses on acquiring sufficient knowledge and a solid emotional education that will enable it to survive and compete in societies with highly complex behaviors in the struggle for dignity, equality, and also for the freedom that allows each person to choose and decide with respect for the dignity, equality, and freedom of others. All of this requires the teaching and learning of these complex social functions or so-called executive functions. These functions essentially require sufficient skills and training to be able to plan and pursue a specific goal or develop behaviors involving a high degree of emotional control, self-control, or cognitive control of oneself. All of these functions must be learned from an early age within the family and at school. There are many studies that amply support what I am saying. Indeed, this book provides many examples and exercises that demonstrate and facilitate this.

Today, we are even beginning to understand the value of these executive functions in relation to learning in areas such as reading, a task that requires, along with many other neural networks, the activity of networks distributed across various areas of the prefrontal cortex (detailed in this book) involved in decision-making and the consequent change of mental strategies. Of particular relevance is the dorsolateral prefrontal cortex (working memory), which allows us to keep in mind what we have just read and thus be able to connect it meaningfully to what follows during reading.

Also relevant is the cingulate cortex, whose activity is coordinated with the emotional brain: emotion, cognition, intention, and action. This is still an open chapter in neurocognitive research.

In any case, this book is of outstanding importance at the present time. It covers everything from the basic concepts of the structure and functioning of the brain to a description of executive functions and their development during the early years of life. This book then moves to its central focus: a wide range of exercises on how to develop concentration, impulse control, executive memory and attention, cognitive flexibility, planning, emotional self-regulation, and many others. All of these topics together paint a vivid picture of the progression of neuroscience in its connection with psychology, education, and the humanities, as well as its enormous impact on the society in which we live. Without a doubt, this book is a valuable work that brings together study and new ideas, which, when put into practice through the exercises proposed by Rafa Guerrero in this book, will yield beneficial results for which we should all be deeply grateful to him. I would like to express my gratitude here.

Francisco Mora
Honorary Professor at the Complutense University
Complutense University of Madrid

AI Usage Statement

DeepL Pro was used to generate a draft translation from the Spanish edition. The text has been subsequently revised.

Introduction

One of the reasons that led me to write this practical book on executive functions is that, after many years of working with children, adolescents, and adults with difficulties in some of their executive functions, such as concentration, planning, or problem solving, many of them found themselves with few serious resources to continue working on executive functions at home. When I was training teachers and professionals, they expressed their frustration at not being able to find a simple, practical manual that included exercises for working on the main executive functions. That is why I decided to write a book that would delve into what executive functions are and, at the same time, offer readers exercises to develop and enhance the executive functions of their children or students.

As a preview for the reader, all the exercises found in this book are designed for a specific age and profile, which is why it is essential to adapt each exercise proposed here. No two children are the same, no two ages are the same, working on executive functions individually is not the same as working on them in a group, and working with a child with learning difficulties or a dysexecutive disorder is not the same as working with a child with no apparent difficulties (neurotypical children).

Another aspect that readers should bear in mind is that there are no exercises or activities that work on a single executive function. For example, there are no exercises designed solely and exclusively to improve concentration. What does exist are exercises that primarily develop concentration, as well as other executive functions. When we work on one executive function, it is very likely that other executive functions that we are not working on directly will also improve considerably. That is why some exercises that have been included in a chapter on a specific executive function could have been included in other chapters as well.

All the activities and exercises proposed in this book have been classified according to the age range at which they can be carried out (see the "Solutions" section). The vast majority of them can be used with children aged 5-6 and above, although some can be used with children aged 3–4 and above, and others that are more complex are suitable for children aged 10–11 and above, or even for teenagers and adults. It is important to note that these ages are always guidelines, as each exercise must be adapted to the situation, difficulty, and history of each child. Therefore, do not take the suggested ages as fixed and rigid: adapt each exercise to the needs of each child and/or group.

Let's be aware of the impact that mothers, fathers, teachers, professionals, and other members of society have on our children. By working on and practicing specific executive functions, we are modifying the brain both structurally and functionally. As Barbara Wilson says, by stimulating and working on executive functions, we are shaping the brains of our children and students.

References

Ratiu, P., Talos, I.-F., Haker, S., Lieberman, D., & Everett, P. (2004). The tale of Phineas Gage, digitally remastered. *Journal of Neurotrauma*, 21(5), 637–643. https://doi.org/10.1089/089771504774129964

Van Horn, J. D., Irimia, A., Torgerson, C. M., Chambers, M. C., Kikinis, R., & Toga, A. W. (2012). Mapping connectivity damage in the case of Phineas Gage. *PLOS ONE*, 7(5), e37454. https://doi.org/10.1371/journal.pone.0037454

Chapter 1

The brain, that great unknown

The brain as a tower of control

What is the brain? We could say that the brain is the control tower where all psychological processes take place. The brain controls our entire body. Thanks to this organ, we are able to enjoy a sunset, solve a quadratic equation, get excited watching a movie, and learn new recipes.

But what do we know about how the brain evolves and develops? In the womb, at around eight weeks of gestation, the brain accounts for 50% of the total body size, which shows the importance of this organ from the earliest stages of life. At around five months of pregnancy, the brain accounts for 14% of the total body weight. This percentage continues to decrease, and the brain of a newborn can weigh around 335 grams (10% of its weight) at the time of birth; this weight is approximately equivalent to that of an adult chimpanzee's brain. It is not that the human brain is the largest of all animals, but rather that it is the best connected. By the first year of life, a child's brain weighs close to 1 kg, which is already close to the average weight of an adult brain (1300–1400 grams).

The specialized cells in the brain are called neurons. Thanks to the connections between these neurons, the brain is capable of learning, feeling emotions, sensing, performing behaviors, and enjoying good company, among many other functions. The connection through which one neuron communicates with another is known as a synapse. It is estimated that the human brain contains a total of 100 billion neurons. Furthermore, to give us an idea of the complexity of the brain and its connections, each neuron establishes a connection (synapse) with between 100 and 100,000 different neurons.

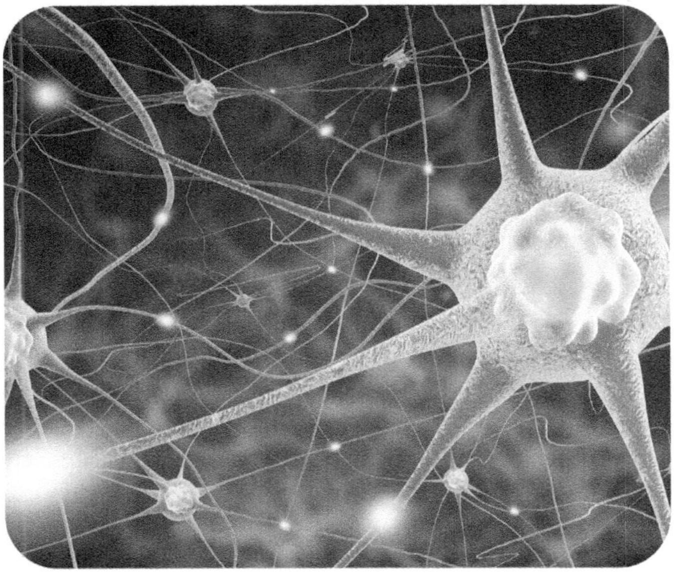

DOI: 10.4324/9781003794332-1

As far as brain metabolism is concerned, we can point out that a child's brain is extremely active throughout childhood. For example, a newborn baby's brain uses around 60% of its total oxygen, while the adult brain uses around 18–20% of the body's total oxygen for brain functions.

There are many myths surrounding the brain and nervous system. One of the most common and widespread neuromyths is that "the bigger the brain, the greater the intelligence." Of course, this is completely false, because intelligence is not simply a matter of having a larger brain, but depends on a greater number of nerve connections. Consider, for example, the brain of a whale, which weighs approximately 7 kg; whale is the animal with the heaviest brain, but are whales more intelligent than humans?

Higher mental functions

Throughout its evolution, the human brain has developed a range of mental functions that distinguish it from the brains of other animal species. These higher mental functions can be classified into four main groups: *gnosis*, *praxis*, language, and executive functions. In this book, we will focus on executive functions, but before doing so, let's take a closer look at all the higher mental functions:

1 **Gnosis:** This refers to the processes involved in perception, through which we can receive information from the environment around us. *Gnosis* integrates the senses of sight, hearing, touch, taste, and smell. We need the senses to develop our brain.

One way to work *on gnosis* with our children is to take photos of everyday objects and cover or cut out some parts. In this case, we would be working on visual *gnosis*, but similar activities can be done with any of the senses. Try to recognize the following objects visually:

2 **Praxias:** These are all the behaviors we engage in, from the most automatic and involuntary, such as reflexes, to the most complex behaviors, such as learning a language or performing a choreographed dance. *Gnosis* and *praxis* are the two basic components of what Piaget called

the *sensorimotor period,* which brings together the processes of receiving stimuli (*gnosis)* and executing behaviors (*praxis)*. The sensorimotor stage spans from birth to approximately 2 years of age.

A simple exercise to work on our children's *praxias*, that is, their motor skills, consists of making the following copies:

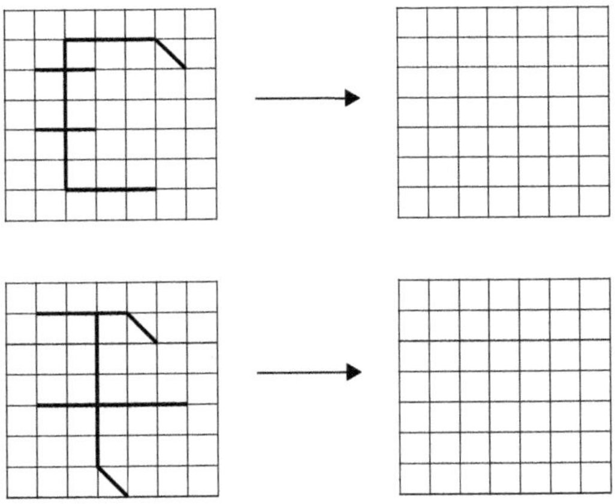

3 **Language:** In the vast majority of children, language usually begins around the age of 2. Thanks to language, we can communicate with our loved ones and friends. We are the only species that has language as such; other species communicate, but they do not have language as we understand it. Within language, we can identify different processes that make it possible: expression, comprehension, writing, reading, discrimination, fluency, vocabulary, etc. All of these can—and should—be reinforced and stimulated. A classic exercise for working on language is hangman. Do you remember when we played hangman as children?

4 **Executive functions:** The first executive functions begin to appear around the age of 2. However, some executive functions tend to develop and become internalized a few years later. For example, impulse inhibition usually begins around the age of 4, which coincides with a proliferation of inhibitory neurons in the child's brain, facilitating the process of impulse inhibition.

Around the age of 6–7, children already have these four higher mental functions available to help them operate and function in their daily lives. This is why Piaget called the stage that begins at this age *the concrete operational stage*, because children already have the four higher mental functions that will allow them to adapt effectively in their daily lives. What kind of actions can a child perform from the age of 6? For example, children are able to do sums, but with external help (an abacus, their fingers, apples, etc.). In contrast, in the *formal operations stage,* which usually begins at age 12, children do not need to see what they are counting, as they can imagine it in their minds. They already have a great capacity for abstraction and reasoning. In both stages, concrete operations and formal operations, good executive functioning is required.

Higher Mental Functions	
Higher mental functions	Acquisition
Gnosis (perception)	0–2 years; sensory-motor period
Praxias (motor)	
Language	From age 2
Executive functions	From 2–4 years

Plasticity of the brain

We can define **brain plasticity** as the set of changes that occur in the central nervous system as a result of learning, training, experience, possible injuries, or degenerative processes in the brain itself. Therefore, brain plasticity is the brain's ability **to change** in response to the demands of an environment that is also changing. Any of us can train and improve our executive functions regardless of our age. It is true that the principle of plasticity indicates that a young brain learns more and better than an older brain, but, in reality, anyone can improve their executive performance through training and practice.

The brain loves surprises, incongruities, and novelty. Brain activation is greater when we encounter a new situation or activity that does not meet our expectations. It is at this moment that our executive functions kick in so that we can respond to the situation in front of us in the most satisfactory way possible. The reason the brain is oriented toward novelty is that it likes to learn new things. However, for learning to occur, the following four requirements are necessary: perception, motivation, attention, and memory. Without these four requirements, there will be no learning. In other words, if we cannot perceive, if we are not motivated to perform the task, if we do not pay attention, or if we do not have a minimum capacity for memory, learning will not occur.

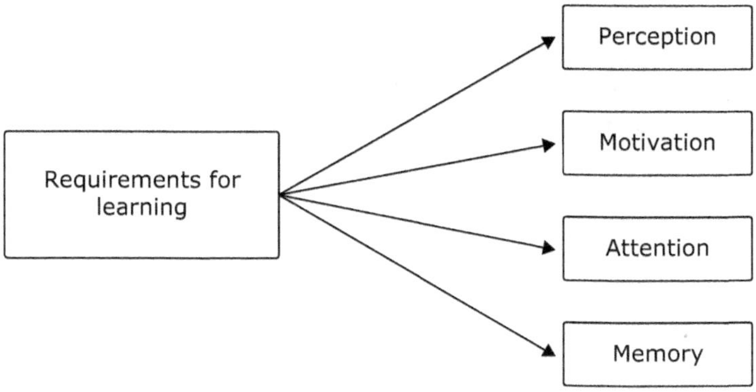

Through training and exercising our executive functions, we can modify the structure and functioning of our nervous system. Many studies show that the brain changes through experience and learning, as well as through training and strengthening executive functions. The brain is like a muscle that we can train, just as we train our bodies when we play sports or go to the gym.

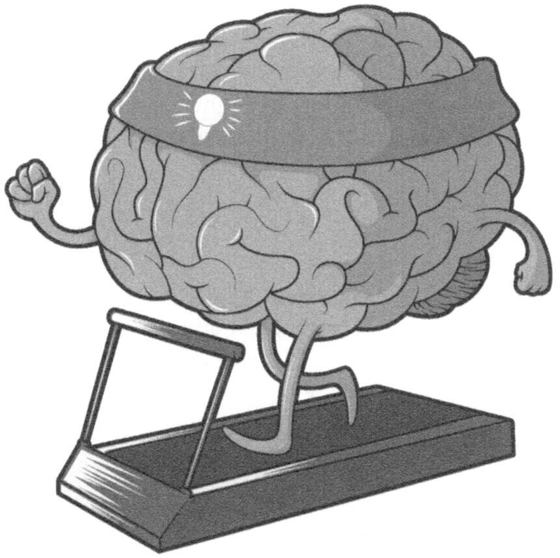

Eleanor Maguire's studies in 2000 highlighted the relevance and effects of neuroplasticity. Maguire compared the hippocampi of London taxi drivers with the hippocampi of people who did not need to memorize so many streets or have excellent spatial orientation. The hippocampus, as we will see in the next chapter, is closely related to memory and spatial orientation. This author concluded that taxi drivers' hippocampi were larger than those of the rest of the population due to their daily training. The nervous system, therefore, can change as a result of learning and training, as well as brain injuries. This occurs at any age.

Other studies have also reached the same conclusions. For example, it has been proven that people who regularly play a musical instrument have an auditory cortex that is 25% more developed. It has also been proven that blind people use their visual cortex, located in the occipital lobe, to read Braille by touch. With all these examples, we can see how the brain adapts to different situations and changes.

Executive functions are located in the frontal lobe, more specifically in the prefrontal cortex, which is located in the anterior part of the frontal lobe. That is why, as we will see in more detail in the chapter on executive function disorders, injuries to the prefrontal cortex can cause difficulties in concentration, impulse control, working memory, planning, and other executive functions. Thanks to brain plasticity, certain injuries or disorders are likely to recover better through executive training.

Reference

Maguire, E. A., Gadian, D. G., Johnsrude, I. S., Good, C. D., Ashburner, J., Frackowiak, R. S. J., & Frith, C. D. (2000). Navigation-related structural change in the hippocampi of taxi drivers. *Proceedings of the National Academy of Sciences of the United States of America*, 97(8), 4398–4403. https://doi.org/10.1073/pnas.070039597

Chapter 2

The four brains

The brain functions holistically, meaning that everything is connected and the different parts of the brain communicate with each other. In this chapter, we will look at the four major areas of the brain and how they communicate with each other to enable a person to function properly. When we talk about four brains, we are using a metaphor. Obviously, we do not have four brains but rather four major areas of the brain. As we discussed in the previous chapter, the brain receives information through the five senses, processes it, and ultimately responds to it. The part of the brain responsible for receiving all the information (impulses, needs, emotions, ideas, thoughts, etc.) and giving a specific response to it is the prefrontal cortex, which corresponds to the fourth brain, which we will discuss below. It is striking—though perhaps not accidental—that the brain develops both phylogenetically and ontogenetically through the same stages, which we will discuss in this chapter. Phylogeny is responsible for studying how a particular species has evolved, while ontogeny studies the development of a particular individual belonging to a particular species from fertilization to death.

Ernst Haeckel's recapitulation theory (1866) argues that child development is a summary of the phylogenetic evolutionary history of our species.

Reptilian brain

The reptilian brain, also known as the primitive brain or reptilian complex, is located at the base of our brain. It is the most archaic and primitive part, with origin dating back some 500 million years. This is the type of brain associated with reptiles such as crocodiles, Komodo dragons, snakes, and lizards.

DOI: 10.4324/9781003794332-2

The two most important structures of the reptilian brain are the brainstem and the cerebellum. The brainstem has functions related to satisfying the following basic needs:

- Hunger
- Thirst
- Reproduction
- Sleep-wake cycle
- Breathing
- Protection
- Attention (arousal)
- Heart rate
- Temperature regulation

The reptilian brain is essential for the survival of the species. This helps explain why the brain stem is already developed by the end of the first trimester of pregnancy. Another important structure of the reptilian complex is the cerebellum, which is closely related to body balance and hearing. Reflexes, needs, and instincts are encoded in the reptilian brain, which is why it is also known as the survival brain or the acting brain. It is not a thinking or sentient brain; rather it only acts in survival situations.

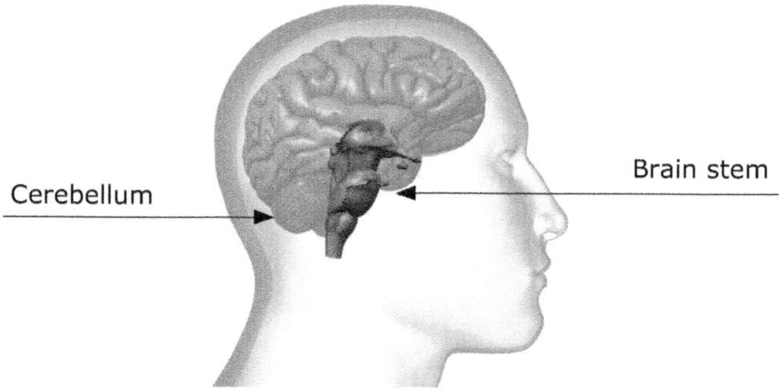

Therefore, the reptilian brain aims to ensure the survival of the species. This structure can produce three basic types of responses, known in English as the three "Fs": *flight, fight, and freeze.* We can translate these into Spanish as huida, ataque, and parálisis. When the brain detects that our life is in danger, it automatically, involuntarily, and unconsciously triggers one of these three responses. This is the part of the brain that is most active in newborns and babies.

The following are the most relevant characteristics of the reptilian complex:

- It is the most archaic part of the brain.
- It is unconscious, involuntary, and automatic.
- It is a reactive brain.
- It does not require learning, as it is an innate brain.
- It is oriented toward the here and now (the present).
- The consequences of an injury to the reptilian complex are more predictable, although the affected person is always in danger of death.

The emotional brain

The emotional brain has its evolutionary origins around 180–200 million years ago, with the appearance of the first mammals on Earth. Located just above the reptilian brain, it is the brain of mammals such as dolphins, giraffes, and elephants.

The emotional brain has five basic functions that differentiate it from the rest of the brain:

- Basic learning
- Memory
- Emotions
- Sociability
- Attachment

Animals that do not have an emotional brain, such as insects and reptiles, do not form attachment relationships with their young or experience emotions. A reptile lays its eggs and does not establish an emotional bond with its offspring. This contrasts with species that have an emotional brain, in which attachment and care for the young play a central role.

Anatomically, the emotional brain is located in the limbic system, which is a set of structures closely related to the functions mentioned above. The emotional brain guides us toward what we find pleasant and away from what we find unpleasant. Its three most important structures are the hypothalamus, the hippocampus, and the amygdala. The amygdala deserves special mention because it is closely related to emotions, especially unpleasant emotions such as fear, anger, sadness, and disgust. For example, learned fears are encoded in the amygdala. When we experience these emotions, the amygdala becomes highly activated. The neural pathway connecting the amygdala to the prefrontal cortex enables a person to regulate their emotions and function effectively.

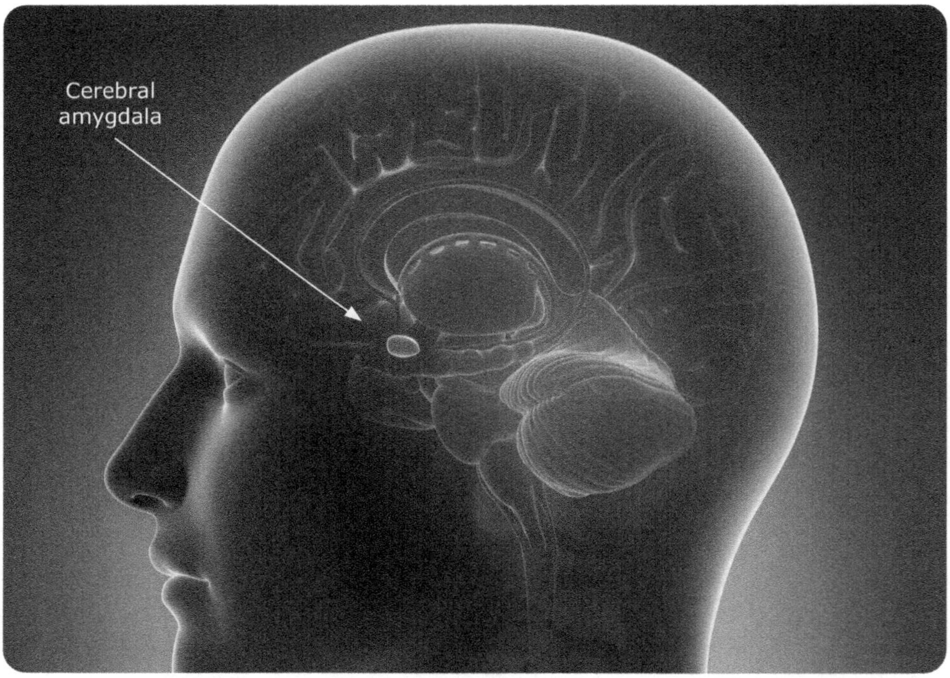

Like the reptilian brain, the emotional brain functions involuntarily, unconsciously, and automatically, meaning that we are not always aware of all the emotions we experience. If the reptilian brain is the brain that acts, the emotional brain is the brain that feels.

The rational brain

Thirdly, we have the rational brain, which is located in the neocortex, the outermost layer of the brain. If we were to open the skull, the first thing we would find is our neocortex. It is the most modern part of the brain and the last to appear, both phylogenetically and ontogenetically, as its development is associated with the emergence of the first primates some 60–65 million years ago. It is our thinking brain, which is why we say it is the brain that thinks. It is also responsible for storing information, as long-term memory is distributed throughout the neocortex.

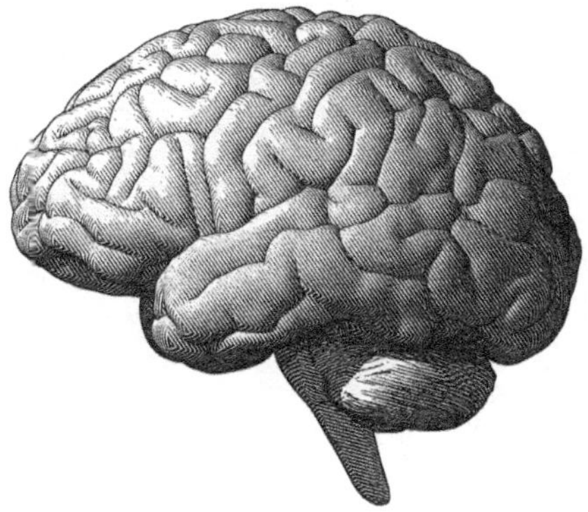

The neocortex is divided into two hemispheres, joined by a bundle of fibers called the corpus callosum. Some studies have suggested that women have a 20% thicker corpus callosum, which indicates greater interconnectivity between the hemispheres and, therefore, greater coordination between them. The hemispheres are divided into four cerebral lobes: occipital, parietal, temporal, and frontal. For the purpose of this book, the frontal lobe is of particular interest, and we will discuss it in greater depth in the following chapters.

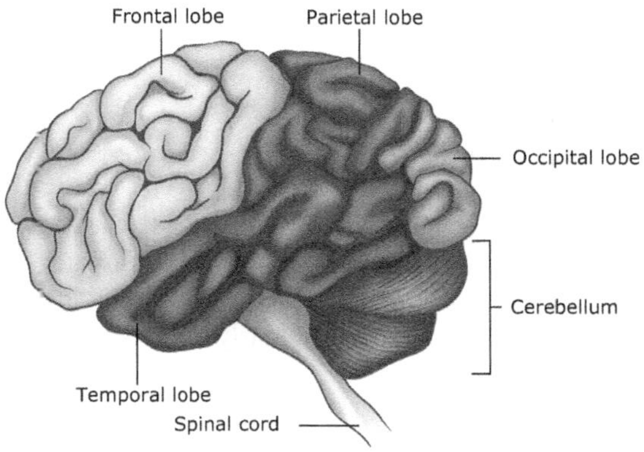

Executive brain

Fourth and last, we have the executive brain. Although this brain is part of the neocortex, given its importance, I have decided to separate them. It is the brain that executes, since the executive brain is located in the prefrontal cortex, the seat of executive functions. Over the last few thousand years, the prefrontal cortex has undergone extraordinary growth in comparison with the rest of the neocortex. This growth has involved not only an expansion of its area but also an increase in the number of neuronal connections in this region. The prefrontal cortex accounts for approximately one-third of the neocortex.

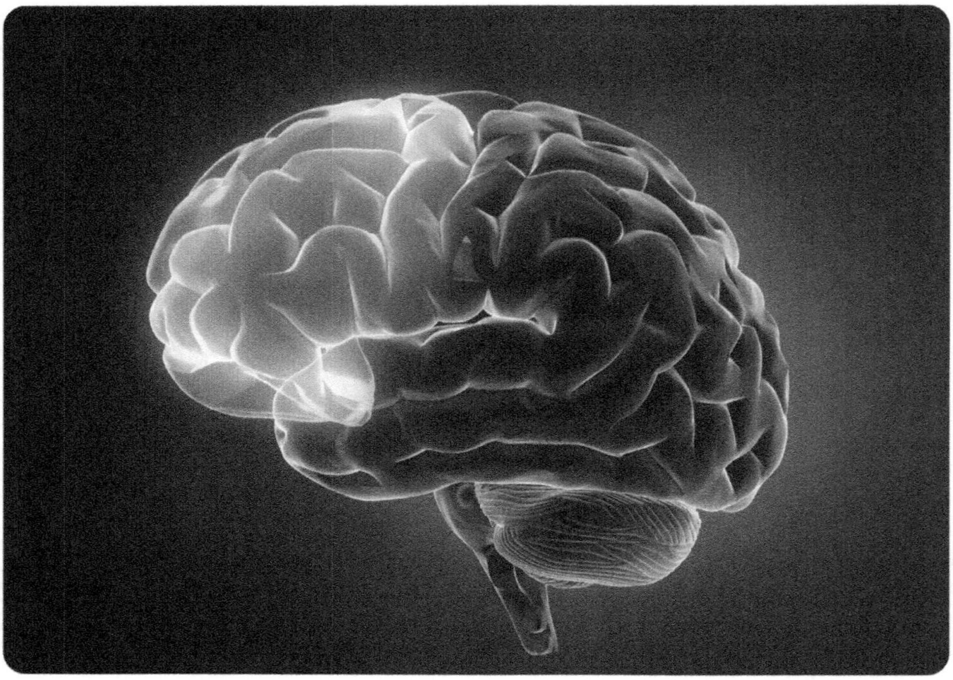

The prefrontal cortex is responsible for executive functions such as planning, working memory, decision-making, inhibitory control, and concentration. When this area is damaged or altered, a person's ability to function executively decreases considerably. Early lesion studies in monkeys found that damage to the frontal lobes could lead to excessive motor activity and reduced concentration. This increased activity and restlessness reflected the loss of a key structure involved in controlling impulses, needs, emotions, and thoughts—the prefrontal cortex.

All executive functions are future-oriented. This is why it is said that the prefrontal cortex opens the organism to the future. It is the brain that executes. All mammals have a neocortex and prefrontal cortex, but only humans have proper executive functions. We sometimes hear that children are very honest and cruel in their comments and actions toward others, but I don't think that's the case. It's not that they are cruel; rather, their prefrontal cortex is not yet sufficiently developed to prevent them from doing or saying things that may hurt or harm others.

We can say that the farther back we are in the brain (posterior brain areas), the more it resembles an Albacete knife, and the farther forward we move (anterior brain areas), the more it resembles a Swiss Army knife. This is because the reptilian brain areas are more rigid and automated, while the rational brain and prefrontal cortex areas are more flexible and controlled. For this reason, when there is an injury, trauma, or tumor in the posterior areas of the brain, its possible consequences can be predicted with greater certainty. In the anterior areas, however, the effects are much more variable and therefore more difficult to anticipate.

The basic characteristics of the prefrontal cortex are as follows:

- It is the most modern layer, both phylogenetically and ontogenetically.
- Conscious, voluntary, and controlled.
- Future-oriented, although it can also think about the present moment and reflect on the past.
- Lesions in the prefrontal cortex cause unpredictable damage.

Conclusions

In conclusion, we could say that the reptilian brain and the emotional brain correspond to a warm brain, while the neocortex and prefrontal cortex correspond to a cold brain. The reptilian brain responds to the here and now, while the rational and executive brains are focused on the future, although they can also think about the past and the present moment. The first two brains are archaic, in that they are simple and ancient, and the rational and executive brains are more avant-garde. If we use the metaphor of a car, the warm brain would be the accelerator, while the cold brain would be in charge of the brakes, that is, the capacity for inhibition and impulse control. For a person to adapt well, it is just as important to know how to use the accelerator as it is to know how to use the brake.

<table>
<tr><th>Brain type</th><th>Basic function</th><th>Location Anatomical</th><th>Time</th><th>Hot brains vs. cold brains</th><th>Car metaphor</th></tr>
<tr><td>Reptilian brain</td><td>Brain that acts</td><td>Brainstem and cerebellum</td><td>Present</td><td rowspan="2">Hot or lower brain</td><td rowspan="2">Car accelerator</td></tr>
<tr><td>Emotional brain</td><td>Brain that feels</td><td>Limbic system</td><td>Present and past</td></tr>
<tr><td>Rational brain</td><td>Thinking brain</td><td>Neocortex</td><td>Present and past</td><td rowspan="2">Cold or higher brain</td><td rowspan="2">Car brake</td></tr>
<tr><td>Executive brain</td><td>Executing brain</td><td>Prefrontal cortex</td><td>Future</td></tr>
</table>

Reference

Haeckel, E. (1866). *Generelle Morphologie der Organismen: Allgemeine Grundzüge der organischen Formen-Wissenschaft, mechanisch begründet durch die von Charles Darwin reformirte Descendenz-Theorie* (2 vols.). Berlin: Georg Reimer.

Chapter 3

What are executive functions?

Read the following story carefully. *Juan is a middle-aged civil guard who is working when he suddenly starts to get a headache. His superior tells him to go home and rest. Juan arrives home and is surprised to find his wife in bed with another man. At that moment, Juan grabs his gun and is about to shoot him when, suddenly, something makes him stop.* Do you know what made him reconsider what he was about to do? His executive functions. Thanks to his well-functioning executive functions, Juan was able to anticipate and assess the future consequences of killing his wife's lover. By being able to visualize them, he was able to stop himself. This is the example that Spanish philosopher and educator José Antonio Marina often uses to explain in a practical way what executive functions are.

In this chapter, we will discuss in detail the different executive functions available to humans. All of them are dimensional, meaning that it is not a question of having them or not having them, but rather that we have a certain amount of each. Metaphorically speaking, executive functions are not a matter of black and white, but rather exist on a gray scale. Depending on how we use them, we will have developed them to a greater or lesser extent.

For example, a child may have very good concentration skills but poor working memory. In contrast, another child may have difficulty concentrating but excellent planning and working memory skills.

Concept

The concept of executive functions was formalized by neuropsychologist Muriel Lezak, although it was Alexander R. Luria, a leading figure of the Soviet school, who highlighted the importance of the prefrontal cortex in people's performance and adaptation. Joaquín Fuster, a psychiatrist and professor at the University of California, Los Angeles (UCLA), has been one of the leading researchers on the prefrontal cortex, which, as we shall see, is central to executive functions.

Historically, phrenologists, led by Franz Joseph Gall, emphasized the importance of the frontal lobe in these types of psychological processes.

DOI: 10.4324/9781003794332-3

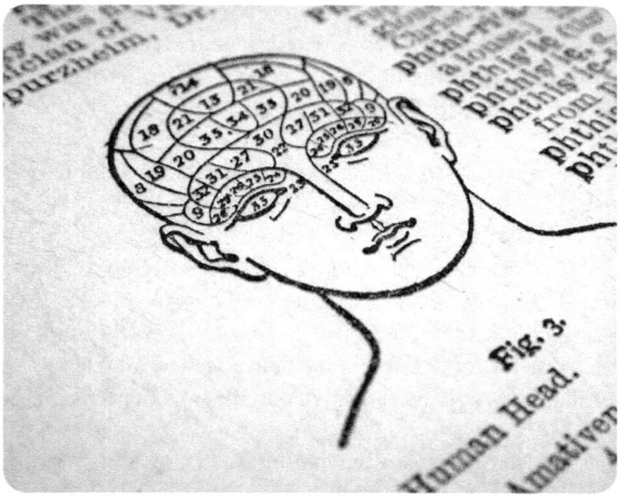

Norman and Shallice argue that there are two types of situations in everyday life: *routine situations*, which are characterized by being automated, and *novel situations*, which require all of our brain resources and are related to executive functions. Executive functions are sometimes also known as *executive intelligence.*

Definition

There are currently a total of 33 different definitions of executive functioning. For this reason, it is difficult to establish a single definition of executive functions. However, the vast majority of definitions have characteristics and aspects in common. Let's look at some of the most representative definitions.

José Antonio Portellano, professor at the Faculty of Psychology of the Complutense University of Madrid, defines executive functions as the mechanism that allows us to solve problems, thanks to their ability to carry out action plans to plan, initiate, direct, and supervise behaviors aimed at achieving objectives.

Ozonoff and his collaborators define executive functions as the cognitive construct used to describe goal-directed, future-oriented behaviors that are considered to be mediated by the frontal lobes. They include planning, response inhibition, flexibility, organized searching, and working memory. All executive functioning behaviors share the need to detach from the immediate environment or external context.

According to Muriel Lezak, who coined this concept, executive functions allow humans to formulate goals, plan objectives, and execute behaviors effectively. The ultimate purpose of executive functions is behavior control.

Russell Barkley, one of the world's leading experts on attention deficit hyperactivity disorder (ADHD), defines executive functions as the ability to act on oneself and improve one's future.

According to Javier Tirapu, one of Spain's leading neuropsychologists, executive functioning is the ability to find solutions to novel problems by predicting the consequences of each imagined solution. He adds that patients with executive problems can solve automated situations but do not know how to solve novel problems.

For the Toledo philosopher José Antonio Marina, executive intelligence is the ability to manage behavior well, choose goals, make use of information, and regulate emotions.

According to Joaquín Fuster, psychiatrist and professor at UCLA, executive functions are those brain functions that enable the organization of actions over time to achieve goals in order to solve problems.

Therefore, as Gazzaniga rightly states, executive functions refer to a set of strategies that include:

a The intention to inhibit a response or delay it over time.
b A strategic plan for action sequences.
c A mental representation of the task that includes information about relevant stimuli encoded in memory and the desired future goal.

Author	*Definition of executive functions*
José Antonio Portellano	A mechanism that enables problem solving, thanks to its ability to implement action plans to plan, initiate, direct, and supervise behaviors aimed at achieving objectives.
Ozonoff et al.	The cognitive construct used to describe behaviors directed toward a goal, oriented toward the future, which are considered to be mediated by the frontal lobes.
Muriel Lezak	They enable humans to formulate goals, plan objectives, and execute behaviors effectively.
Russell Barkley	Ability to act on oneself and improve the future.
Javier Tirapu	Ability to find solutions to novel problems, predicting the consequences of each imagined solution.
José Antonio Marina	Ability to manage behavior effectively, choose goals, make use of information, and regulate emotions.
Joaquín Fuster	Those brain functions that enable the organization of actions over time to achieve goals and solve problems.

Characteristics

Executive functions are one of the characteristics that differentiate us from other animal species. We could say that the prefrontal area, where executive functions are primarily located, is the *center of humanity*. The vast majority of executive functions are future-oriented. Thus, other animals do not engage in behaviors to obtain results in the future, especially in the medium or long term. For example, humans buy a cake to eat on their child's birthday, which will be celebrated in a few days; they organize summer well in advance; they take out mortgages; they pursue university degrees that take at least four years; and they write doctoral theses that require a great deal of effort and time. In short, we invest time. This is something exclusively human.

Good executive functioning is the result of learning, practice, and experience. Executive functions are not genetically determined, which is good news because if a child performs poorly in any executive function, they can be trained. Executive functions are most developed at home, at school, and through social relationships (friends, sports, etc.). We know that training and practice can modify both the anatomy and functioning of the prefrontal cortex.

Studies have shown that children with higher intelligence activate less of their brain when performing a given task. In other words, a child with an intellectual disability needs to activate more areas of the brain and spend more time on a given task.

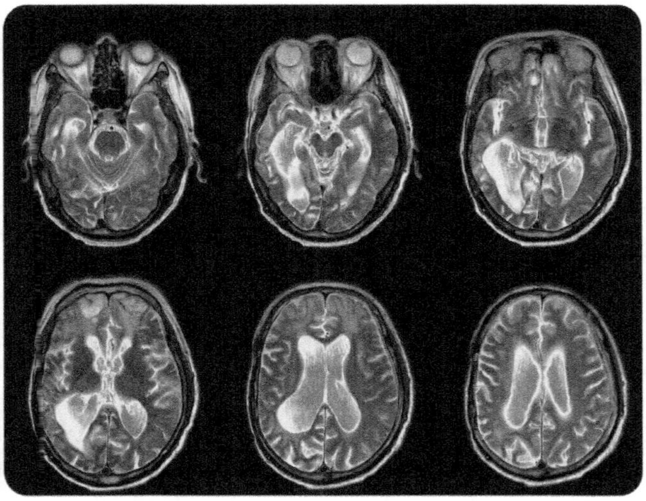

The metaphor of the conductor of orchestra

Many metaphors and similes have been used to describe executive functions' role in people's lives: the conductor of an orchestra, the helm of a ship, the head of a company, etc. One of the most commonly used metaphors is that of the orchestra conductor, devised by Goldberg.

Imagine you have gone to see a classical music concert. Who do you think is more important for everything to go well? The musicians or the conductor? Both are essential for us to enjoy beautiful symphonies. Each musician and each of the different sections must play in a coordinated manner: wind section, string section, percussion section, etc. But it is also important that the person who coordinates them all (the conductor) does their job well. If we understand the different sections of the orchestra as the different parts of the brain and the conductor as the executive functions, we will understand this metaphor well. The prefrontal cortex, which governs executive functions, receives all the information from the rest of the brain (impulses, needs, emotions, thoughts, etc.) and makes a decision that will be as adaptive as possible. This is what we call executive functioning.

In short, and continuing with the similes, executive functions act as an executive, a manager, and a distributor. *Executive*, because they allow us to set goals and strategies to achieve them; *manager*, because they allow us to evaluate the consequences of our actions when solving problems or conflicts; and *distributor*, because they distribute tasks among the neural networks involved.

Main functions of executive functions

Now that we know what executive functions are and what their role is in the brain, we will focus on the different types of executive functions that exist. A total of 32 executive functions have been identified. Generally, executive functions are classified into two types:

- **Cool executive functions:** These types of executive functions are activated when emotions are not intense or are easily controllable. For example, if we have to decide which car to buy, it is important that we do so when we are calm, so that we can activate cold executive functions: concentration (which cars we like), reasoning (the pros and cons of each option), working memory (calculating what we can and cannot afford), decision making (which car to choose), etc.

- **Warm or hot executive functions:** These are activated when we need to exercise significant self-control over the emotions we are experiencing at a given moment. For example, when faced with a heated argument with a friend or partner, we need to activate our warm or hot executive functions to avoid saying or doing things that we may later regret, or things that are maladaptive for ourselves or others. In this situation, it is essential to have emotional regulation strategies in place. When we discussed the four brains in the previous chapter, we said that emotions originate in the limbic system (emotional brain), but we also said that emotions are controlled or managed by executive functions (prefrontal cortex).

The following diagram shows the classification of executive functions (cool vs. warm) and some of the most representative executive functions in both groups.

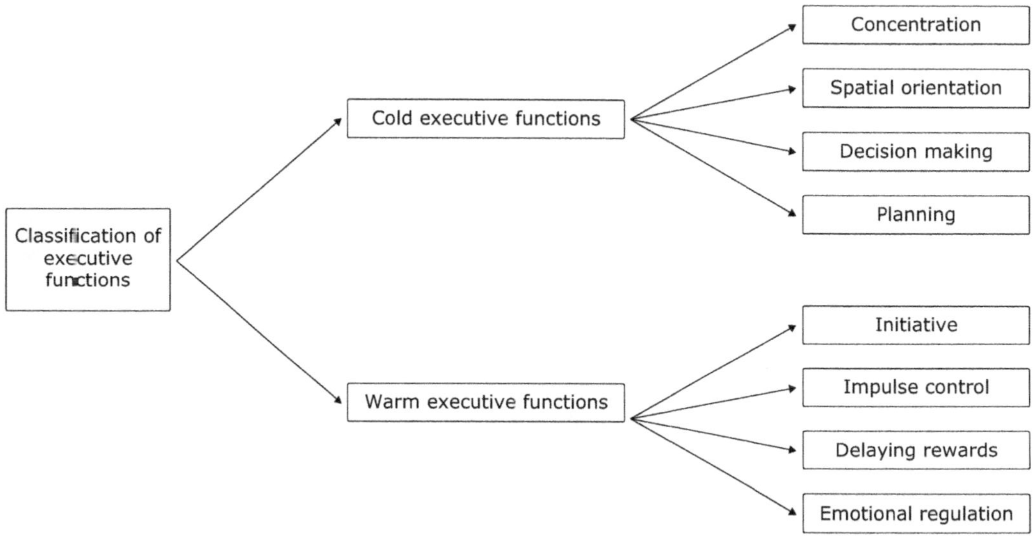

Some of the executive functions most commonly used in intervention programs are as follows:

- Concentration
- Inhibition or impulse control
- Cognitive flexibility
- Emotional self-regulation
- Working memory
- Planning
- Processing speed
- Anticipation
- Spatial orientation
- Delaying rewards
- Reasoning
- Initiative
- Monitoring
- Decision making
- Goal setting
- Metacognition
- Ethical awareness

Despite the large number of executive functions, according to Joaquín Fuster, the five most relevant are the following: concentration, impulse control, working memory, planning, and cognitive flexibility. In this book, in addition to focusing on these five basic executive functions proposed by Fuster, we will explore several others that may be useful to develop in our children and students. All of them will be explained in detail in the following chapters.

Location of executive functions

As we have already mentioned, executive functions are located in the frontal lobe and, specifically, in the prefrontal cortex. Of the four lobes of the brain, the frontal lobe is the most important both anatomically and functionally, as it receives all the information from the other lobes and manages it.

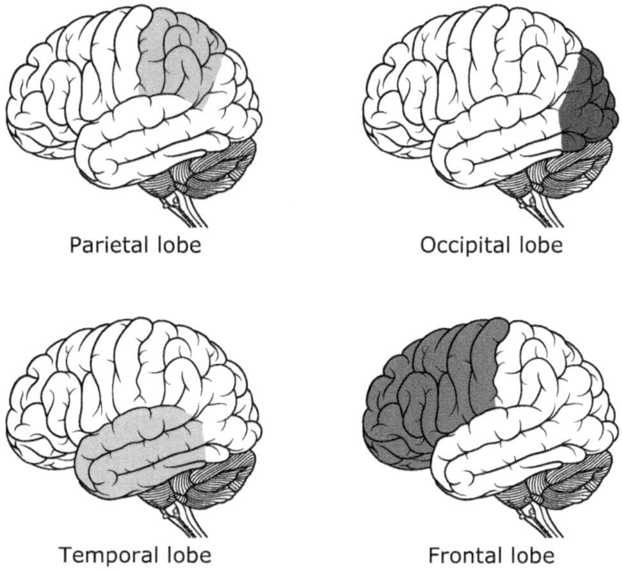

The basic function of the frontal lobe is to coordinate and supervise the functioning of the rest of the brain, i.e., to perform executive functions. In humans, the frontal lobe accounts for one-third of the total brain. In other species, it accounts for much smaller proportions. For example, to give us an idea, the frontal lobe accounts for 17% of the brain in chimpanzees and 7% in dogs. Below we can see the proportion of the brain occupied by the frontal lobe in different species.

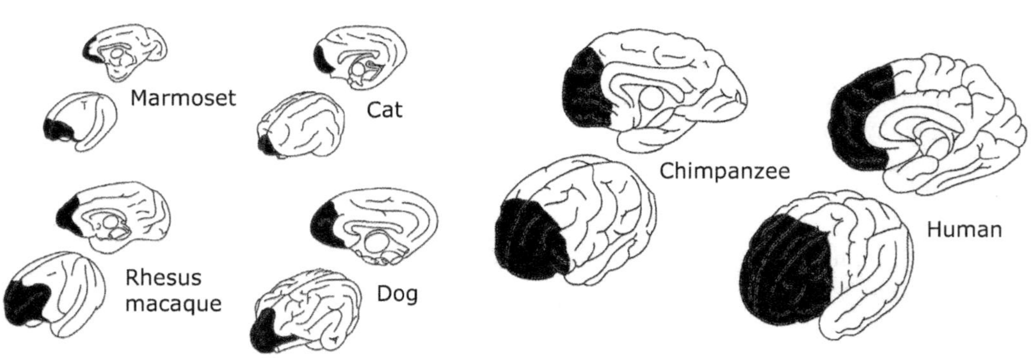

All mammals have a frontal lobe and a prefrontal cortex, but only humans have executive functions. As we have already discussed, the prefrontal cortex is mainly activated when the action we are about to perform is complex or novel. For example, our prefrontal cortex was highly active on the first day we took a practical driving lesson.

At that moment, the task of driving was a great challenge for us, as we had to pay attention to the steering wheel, the gears, the turn signals, the instructor's instructions, and the other cars and pedestrians on the road.

Wasn't it stressful at first? Once we gain experience, we are able to automate these behaviors and, therefore, our prefrontal cortex is barely active, as the action is no longer complex and novel.

Now let's think about the great effort babies must make to learn to walk, preschoolers must make to learn to hold a pencil, and elementary school children must make to balance on a skateboard. In these cases, at first, the prefrontal cortex is highly active, since each activity is novel and requires all the energy.

In conclusion, we can say that for a behavior or skill to become automatic, it is essential to repeat and perform it many times. A behavior becomes automatic only through practice and training. Therefore, it could be said that all automated behaviors were previously controlled behaviors, but not all controlled behaviors become automatic processes. If a task is controlled, it implies that it is novel and, therefore, requires our executive functions. However, tasks that are already automated barely require the activation of our prefrontal cortex.

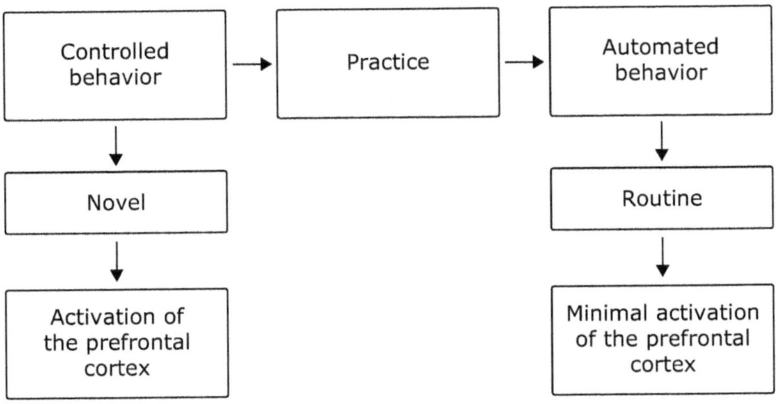

Parts of the prefrontal cortex

As we have already mentioned, executive functions are located in the frontal lobe and, specifically, in the prefrontal cortex. This area is extremely complex and can be divided into three regions with specific functions that are highly relevant to proper executive functioning: the dorsolateral prefrontal cortex, the orbitofrontal cortex, and the medial prefrontal cortex.

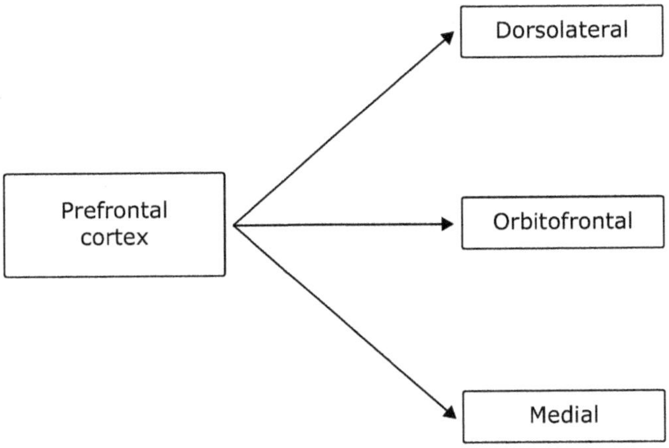

- **Dorsolateral prefrontal cortex:** Its main function is to pursue objectives and goals, allowing us to persevere in a given task. It maintains stimulation and motivation directed toward a goal. It is responsible for executive functions such as planning, working memory, concentration, and cognitive flexibility. Lesions in the dorsolateral prefrontal cortex cause major problems with planning and concentration; in such cases, individuals live only in the present moment and have difficulty anticipating the future and learning from the past.

- **Orbitofrontal cortex:** This structure is located at the base of the frontal lobes and just above the eyes, hence its name (orbitofrontal). It is responsible for controlling interference and stimuli that try to distract us from the task we are doing. It is closely related to the executive function of impulse control. That is why it is said to be related to the management of emotional processes, as it is connected to the limbic system. The main function of the orbitofrontal cortex is to enable the dorsolateral cortex to achieve its goal. Therefore, both are complementary. For example, even though I feel like going to the bathroom, I must not go now. Lesions in the orbitofrontal cortex cause impulsivity, disinhibition, aggressiveness, poor ethical awareness, etc.
- **Medial prefrontal cortex:** This region is related to the nucleus accumbens, which is the pleasure center. Whenever we do something fun, these centers are activated. They seek rewards and identify what can help us remain motivated and focused on what we are doing. Lesions in the medial prefrontal cortex cause apathy, loss of initiative, reduced spontaneous activity, low curiosity, slow processing speed, etc.

Chapter 4

Development of executive functions

Evolutionary development of the frontal lobe

Historically, the frontal lobes have been considered a basic element in measuring the complex cognitive abilities associated with childhood and adolescence. These abilities serve as precursors to psychosocial adjustment and adaptation to adult life.

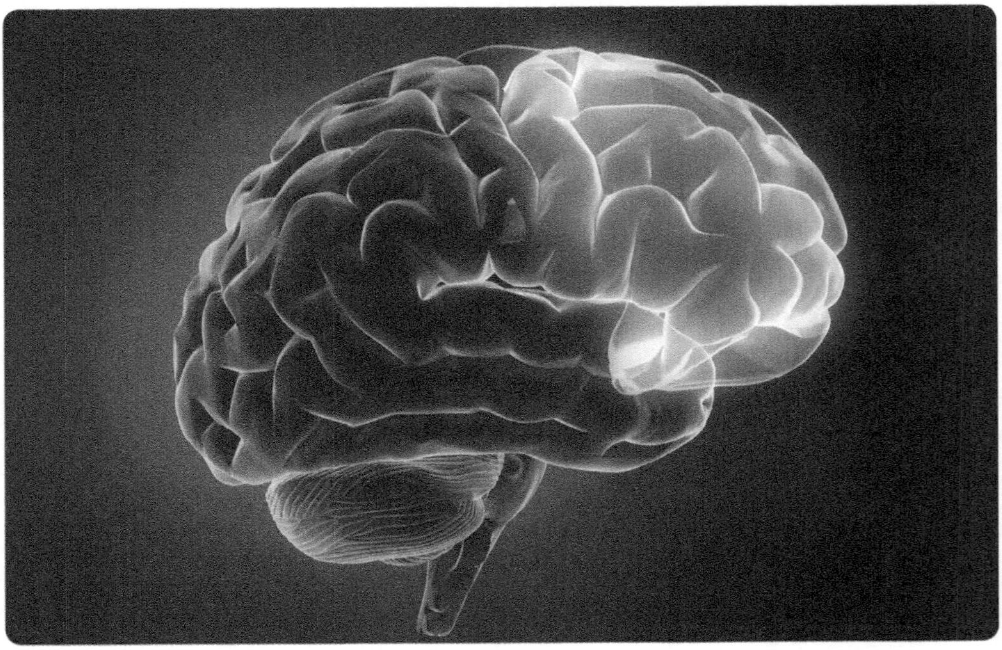

Brain development and growth begin in the womb and progress slowly and gradually. Initially, the areas of the brain that develop most are the sensory and motor areas—coinciding with Jean Piaget's sensorimotor stage—which correspond to the first two years of a child's life. In these early years, the cognitive functions belonging to the child's cerebral cortex develop very little. Although the prefrontal cortex is barely active in the first two years of life, there are some behaviors in babies that lead us to believe that certain basic executive processes already exist. For example, a baby of about seven to eight months is already capable of looking for a toy that has been hidden.

DOI: 10.4324/9781003794332-4

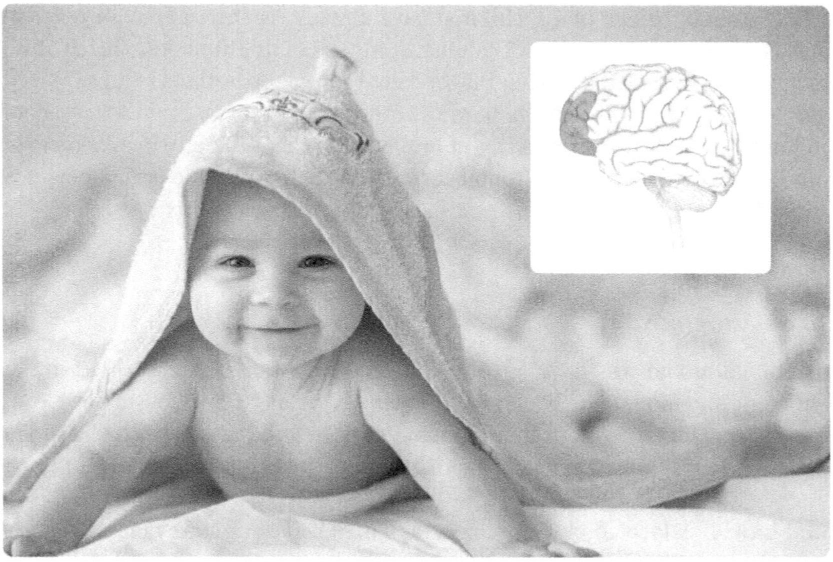

The vast majority of functions associated with the frontal lobes, such as impulse inhibition and planning, among others, reach their peak development between the ages of 4 and 8. Other significant peaks in brain development occur between the ages of 10 and 12 and between 16 and 19. However, these peaks do not involve only growth in the frontal lobe; they also involve increased myelination and synaptogenesis, i.e., the amount of myelin covering the neurons increases and new synaptic connections are formed between neuronal groups. What differentiates humans from other species in terms of the brain is not only related to the size of the lobes and the prefrontal cortex, but also to the neural connectivity between different parts of the brain.

As discussed, certain executive functions do not appear until late childhood, such as impulse inhibition, focused attention (concentration), and planning.

We could say that, around the age of 10, children have already reached a level of performance and execution that is quite similar to that of adults. Some executive functions reach this level around the age of 12, when the stage that Jean Piaget called formal operations begins.

To conclude this section, when do you think we can consider that the brain has reached full maturity? Well, a human brain reaches maturity at around 25 years of age, which shows us how slowly our nervous system evolves. The prefrontal cortex is the last part of the brain to mature. The brain develops from the back to the front: the reptilian complex develops first, and the prefrontal cortex is the last to mature.

Functional three-unit model

The three-unit functional model was developed by Alexander R. Luria, as discussed in the previous chapter. Although this model has been in use for many years, it provides a simple way to understand three basic functional areas of the brain and their specific roles. The same model has been used to explain the four brains. Let's take a closer look at these functional units of the brain.

- **First functional unit:** It is located in the brain stem, which is the structure that acts as a bridge between the brain and the spinal cord. The functions of the brain stem are related to survival and arousal. Arousal is the level of activation we have at a given moment in the day. For example, if we are about to take an exam or a job interview, our level of arousal would be high or very high. However, if we are watching a movie that bores us and we are about to fall asleep in the theater, our level of activation or arousal is minimal. The level of arousal is never non-existent, except in death.

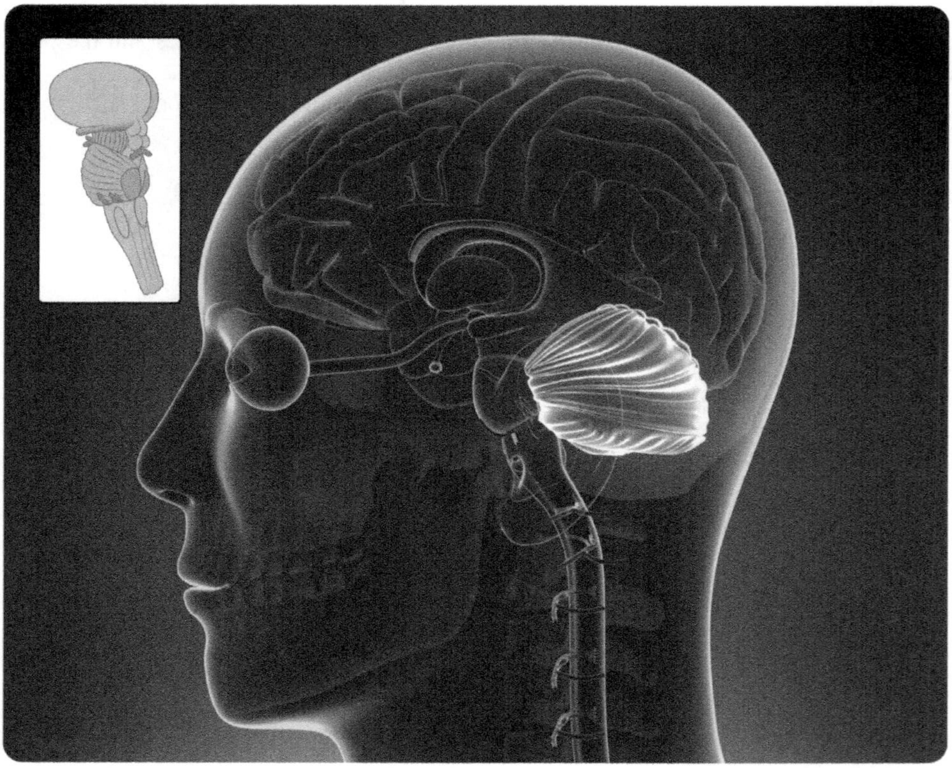

- **Second functional unit:** This unit is related to the process of receiving, analyzing, and storing information. It is located in the cerebral cortex, specifically in the temporal, parietal, and occipital lobes. These three lobes essentially store all kinds of information: memories from our childhood, concepts, sensations, smells, etc. In short, they store our long-term memory.
- **Third functional unit:** This unit is located in the frontal lobes, where executive functions reside. Its purpose is to program, regulate, and evaluate the behavior or activity we are carrying out. It receives information from the other two functional units.

For example, to complete a Sudoku puzzle, we need a minimum level of arousal (first functional unit), information on how to do a Sudoku puzzle correctly, as well as procedural strategies (second functional unit), and the executive functions that would correspond to the third functional unit.

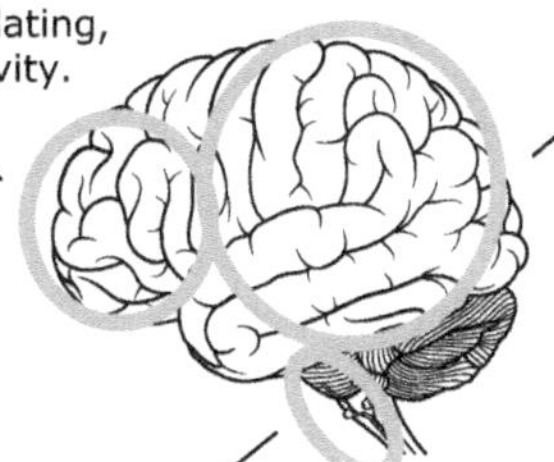

Activation of executive functions

Once we understand the concept of executive functions, let's look at the situations and moments in which these functions are activated, that is, what situations or tasks require us to activate executive functioning. We can say that a person's executive functions are activated in the following six situations:

1 **Faced with novelty:** Any new situation involves the activation of executive functions. For example, when we arrive in a new city, we activate our concentration, spatial orientation, working memory, etc.; in short, our executive functioning. Another everyday example occurs when we buy a new cell phone or computer. Since there is no habitual response to something new, we must be very attentive to the resources we need to adapt as best as possible to the new

environment or stimulus. Once we have become familiar with the city, the level of activation of the prefrontal cortex decreases until a new stimulus appears. If the action becomes automatic through practice, the prefrontal cortex is not activated as much as it was when the task was new.

2 **Maintaining and retrieving information:** Sometimes we need to retrieve information from the past in order to perform a task or behavior correctly. For example, we can retrieve from our long-term memory the meal we made for our friends a few weeks ago that they liked so much.

3 **When initiating or interrupting a behavior:** Whenever we initiate a behavior or interrupt it to do something else, we need executive functioning. This is most evident in complex or novel behaviors. For example, if we are driving on the highway and miss our exit, we must make a U-turn, which requires our full attention.

4 **Coordinating actions:** When we have to perform two or three tasks simultaneously, executive functions are activated to enable us to perform adequately. Imagine that you are cooking dinner and, at the same time, keeping an eye on your child's homework and the phone because a family member is going to call you. Wouldn't your executive functioning be at its peak?

5 **Monitoring action:** When we are aware of what we are doing and how we are doing it, we are monitoring that behavior. In this way, we are able to correct our mistakes and anticipate other possible errors; we are evaluating what we are doing *in real time*, in the present moment.

6 **Following the rules:** We usually have to comply with a series of rules or obligations and, therefore, we must control or postpone our impulses or emotions. So, for example, when your boss tells you off, you probably feel like saying a few things to them, but you limit yourself to following the basic rules of good manners and not exploding as you would really like to.

Chapter 5

Exercises to develop concentration

What is concentration?

We can define concentration as an executive function through which we focus our resources on a specific stimulus, person, activity, or task. Consider the following questions: How many stimuli in the place where you are can you pay attention to right now? Can you focus on all of them or only a few? Can we pay attention to things we are not seeing at this moment? For example, can you remember where you were last summer? And what did you do on your last birthday? As you can see, we can pay attention to both external and internal stimuli (thoughts, memories, anticipation of future possibilities, etc.). In both cases (attention directed both inward and outward), a minimum level of activation is necessary in order to perform the task adequately. We call this activation arousal.

I like to use the metaphor of a spotlight to explain how attention works. Imagine we only have one spotlight to illuminate everything that interests us. There are many stimuli, things, and people around us. Sometimes we will be the ones looking for a particular stimulus with the spotlight, but at other times, it will be the stimulus that catches our attention. The problem with the spotlight is that it is a limited resource. It cannot illuminate everything at once. That is why the spotlight will allow us to pay attention to what it is illuminating, but what is in the shadows cannot be attended to, at least at that moment.

DOI: 10.4324/9781003794332-5

The spotlight metaphor shows us that attentional resources are limited: we cannot attend to all stimuli simultaneously, but must instead filter or select the stimulus or task that most interests, motivates, or rewards us. Although we will look at some pathologies and disorders of executive functions later on, at this point, I would like to point out that children and young people with attention deficit hyperactivity disorder (ADHD) do not lack focus; of course, they have it. Their main difficulty is that they are constantly changing the focus of their attention, which makes it extremely difficult for them to concentrate. It is more a problem of impulse inhibition than concentration. We will explain all this later.

Types of attention

Now that we have seen the metaphor of the spotlight and understood how attention works, we will focus on learning about the different ways of using that spotlight, that is, the different types of attention that exist.

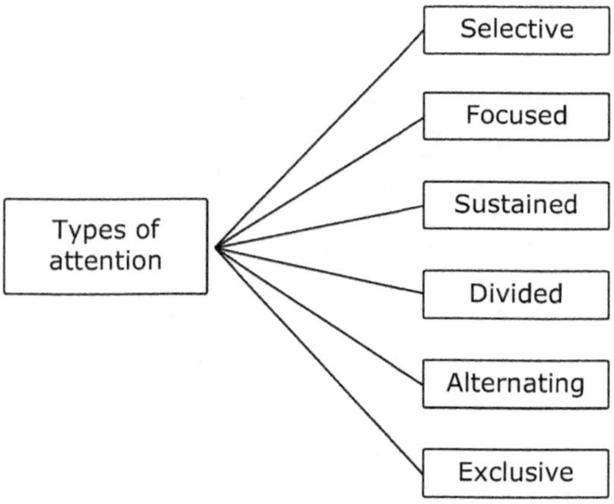

- Selective Attention: We use selective attention when a task or activity requires us to select a specific stimulus from our environment, that is, we select relevant information and inhibit irrelevant stimuli. For example, searching for vowels in a word search or identifying your uncle—whom you have gone to pick up at the train station—are activities that require selective attention.

- Focused Attention: When we concentrate or focus on a specific activity, we are engaging in focused attention. We can focus our attention on visual, auditory, or tactile stimuli. For example, calculating the following mathematical expression requires us to focus our attention:

  2 + 4-1 + 2

- Sustained Attention: This is the ability to consciously maintain an activity for a prolonged period of time. It is also known as sustained attention or executive attention. It is the continuation of focused attention. What differentiates one from the other is the duration of the task, not the type of task. Continuing with the example of focused attention, if instead of doing a single mathematical calculation we had to do a whole sheet, then it would no longer be focused attention but an activity of sustained attention, because it would require persistent attention over time. Other tasks that require sustained attention are reading for half an hour, watching a movie, doing a Sudoku puzzle, or studying for tomorrow's exam. When we have this type of attention active, we say that we are concentrated. Concentration requires willpower, awareness, and perseverance. It is true that sustained attention is more elaborate and difficult when the task is unmotivating and monotonous for the child, since it requires greater effort.

- Divided Attention: In this type of attention, we are performing two or more tasks simultaneously. For example, while we are putting a load of laundry in the washing machine, we are drinking coffee and talking to our friend. In order for divided attention to occur, one of the tasks must be automated, because it is impossible to do two new tasks at the same time.

- Alternating Attention: In alternating attention, we shift our focus when a signal for change is given. We could say that it is the ability that allows us to shift our focus of attention between two or more tasks that require different cognitive responses on our part. For example, we are doing some addition exercises on a sheet of paper, but when we hear a clap or a whistle, we have to switch to the subtraction sheet. It requires two or more tasks, but not simultaneously.
- Exclusive Attention: It is also known as inhibitory attention because the person needs to control (not say or do) a certain behavior that is automatic. This type of attention is clearly reflected in the *Stroop effect*, which we will see in the chapter on impulse control. As you can see, this type of attention is closely related to impulse control or inhibition. Remember when we played "the opposite world" as children? We had to pay attention and control what we were thinking in order to say the exact opposite. That is exclusive attention.

Is being attentive the same as being focused or concentrated?

If you notice, so far we have been using the concepts of attention and concentration as synonyms, but do they refer to the same thing or are there differences between them? To tell the truth, there are differences. In terms of *location*, we can say that the vast majority of attention processes activate posterior areas of the brain, that is, what we called the reptilian brain in Chapter 2. Here we are talking more about attention and arousal. Concentration or executive attention, on the other hand, is located in the frontal areas of the brain, specifically in the prefrontal cortex. Concentration requires willpower, awareness, and perseverance, which does not imply that the task has to be enjoyable or motivating. Sometimes children concentrate on their homework and studies not because they like what they are studying, but because they do not want to be scolded by their parents or because they want to complete their tasks. This does not exclude it from being an executive task (concentration), since they have voluntarily decided to study (they could have refused) and are conscious and persevering in what they do.

Another important difference between attention and concentration, following the metaphor of focus, is that attention is passive, since it is the stimulus or situation that captures my attention, while concentration plays a more active role, since we are the ones who consciously and persistently seek out the stimulus. Let's look at the following example to fully understand the difference between the two. If one day, while walking down the street, I come across a man dressed as the Pink Panther, regardless of my will, he will catch my attention. Therefore, it is the stimulus that captures me and not the other way around. On the other hand, if one day I decide to go out looking for people dressed as the Pink Panther, it will be an exercise in concentration, since I am the one seeking out the stimulus. In the latter case, I am aware of what I am looking for and I am persistent, as well as voluntarily deciding to engage in that behavior.

Finally, it is important to note that concentration is closely related to motivation, curiosity, and expectations. It is easy to pay attention when faced with motivating tasks, but when faced with activities that we find boring and monotonous, it becomes much more difficult to maintain our concentration.

	Brain location	*Active vs. passive*	*Characteristics*
Attention	Posterior areas (reptilian brain)	Passive: the stimulus captures the person's attention	Unconscious Involuntary Changes depending on the stimulus
Concentration	Frontal areas (prefrontal cortex)	Active: the person seeks out and persists with the stimulus or task	Conscious Voluntary Persevering

Evolutionary development of attention

We know that attention is a psychological process that is trained and improved throughout our evolutionary development. In the first year of life, babies learn to control their attention, thanks to their attachment figures (mother, father, and teachers). Every time a baby sees something that interests them and is novel, it will try to focus on it. We must bear in mind that babies and young children have their reptilian brains, that is, their survival brains, active most of the day. This is why babies' attention is reactive, involuntary, unconscious, and with little control. It is stimuli that capture the baby's attention, not the other way around. The areas of the brain that are activated at these ages are the posterior ones.

Gradually, young children's reactive attention will transform into controlled or executive attention, which is what we know as concentration. In this case, the frontal regions of the brain will be activated. For this to happen, it is essential that parents and teachers provide good stimulation and reinforcement. We only achieve controlled attention (concentration) through practice and training.

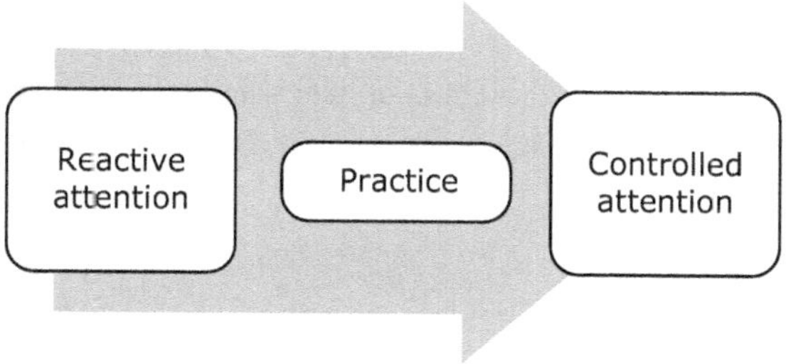

Scientific studies conclude that when we perform an executive task, that is, when we pay attention to something, our heart rate and motor activity decrease significantly. Think, for example, about when you are watching a movie or cooking. When you are concentrating, your heart rate and motor activity decrease. On the other hand, if a stimulus appears at that moment that distracts us, such as someone calling us or hearing a shout, then our heart rate will increase, as will our motor activity.

At around 6 months of age, babies are able to anticipate a situation; that is, they maintain their attention because they know something is about to happen. For example, this occurs in six-month-old babies when they play peek-a-boo with their parents. The novel and unexpected always involuntarily captures the attention of babies (and everyone else). As the brilliant Francisco Mora says, if we were at a conference and a giraffe appeared behind the speaker, we would involuntarily stop paying attention to the speaker because the giraffe captures our attention as it is an unexpected and novel element.

When children are between the ages of 3 and 6, they learn to control their attention and behavior. This is due to the proliferation of inhibitory neurons in the brain, which allows their ability to control and inhibit impulses to develop. At the brain level, the neurotransmitter related to attention and concentration processes is dopamine.

In the following, we will look at ten suggested exercises for working on concentration. Some of the exercises are aimed at younger children in early childhood education, while others, which are more complex, are intended for primary and secondary school students and even adults. It is important to bear in mind that we must adapt the exercises to the profile and difficulties of the person we are working with.

Exercise 1: The imperial eagle

In the following, you will find a table with many animals and objects. Take a good look at the eagle that appears as a model. You must review the table from left to right and from top to bottom, and every time you see the eagle, stomp your foot on the floor.

Ready? Go ahead.

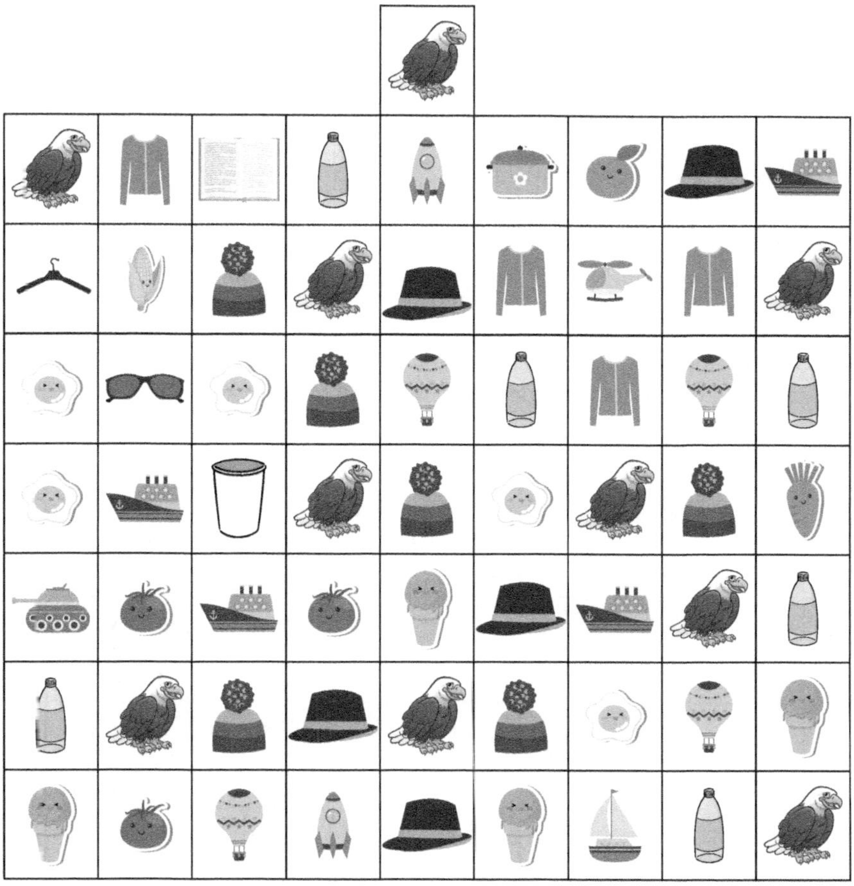

Exercise 2: In search of the lost vowels

In this large word search, you must cross out the lowercase vowels you find. As you can see, it is a long task that will take time, so we will work on selective and sustained attention. Remember that you must cross out the lowercase vowels. And be careful, because there are other types of letters and there are also uppercase letters. Go for it!

J	g	i	m	L	u	y	B	e	Q	and	I
B	a	f	b	n	a	i	N	B	T	U	u
G	Q	q	f	j	J	A	b	A	y	d	c
r	j	u	L	E	T	a	h	G	I	G	f
a	t	H	M	e	I	i	d	I	J	t	N
h	I	J	B	U	F	L	J	i	Q	r	e
b	i	q	a	R	j	d	A	f	e	U	q
Q	a	t	i	H	t	e	n	u	j	y	n

A	m	R	u	d	B	m	r	T	F	i	u
f	e	d	B	N	q	d	q	i	d	j	l
h	M	l	a	u	h	M	l	j	a	A	n
B	Y	F	H	L	J	N	t	R	l	F	L
u	Q	y	b	D	M	E	e	A	m	q	D

Exercise 3: The letter game

In the odd rows, circle all the consonants you find, and in the even rows, cross out the vowels that are preceded and followed by consonants. Concentrate hard!

N	X	E	A	P	W	H	V	A	Q	H	R	Y	A	K	0	G	M	A	Z	L	Q
A	F	Z	R	U	A	I	I	I	S	C	X	I	P	W	B	A	Q	B	D	G	A
Q	I	0	G	A	V	K	Y	D	U	A	A	B	Z	T	P	J	A	L	R	M	C
B	A	L	P	K	R	A	J	E	I	0	Z	H	V	X	A	Q	F	W	S	A	U
T	J	S	A	F	M	Z	V	A	K	L	B	U	A	R	I	H	P	A	0	B	X
F	N	R	E	W	C	A	H	T	Y	Q	M	J	S	S	T	Z	V	K	I	G	L
U	A	I	Z	X	A	0	B	I	I	T	G	P	Y	C	W	A	E	R	H	A	N
L	V	A	J	P	S	R	K	I	A	B	N	A	F	X	U	M	Q	D	A	C	W
0	K	Q	D	C	M	H	W	G	B	V	R	S	B	I	L	Z	T	Y	F	U	J
Y	Z	A	U	T	I	G	T	S	A	J	0	A	D	P	H	N	R	M	A	E	V
E	A	W	H	R	A	L	T	B	M	D	V	I	G	0	S	A	K	U	X	A	P
R	T	P	Y	N	K	A	S	W	L	U	C	Q	E	H	A	F	B	J	0	Z	I
H	B	K	A	G	0	C	E	A	P	R	I	W	A	U	Q	L	D	A	T	S	Y
D	A	J	S	I	L	A	N	F	R	E	P	C	H	V	A	0	G	T	B	A	K
C	Q	T	B	A	E	W	0	R	J	A	A	L	I	M	D	S	T	H	G	K	F
A	L	G	I	D	A	S	M	B	I	H	R	U	E	J	A	0	F	P	C	N	A
S	E	H	A	B	W	I	P	A	G	Z	I	K	A	Q	Y	R	C	A	U	I	M

Exercise 4: Clap your hands

Next, you will see different geometric shapes. Every time you see a geometric shape with four sides, you must clap your hands once. If you see a shape with six sides, you must clap your hands twice. Understood? Let's get started.

Exercise 5: Attention ping-pong

In this exercise, your task is to compare letters and numbers in two columns and identify those that are missing in the adjacent column. Which number or letter is left unpaired? Let's look at an example to understand it better.

Example	W I (B) P X	W P X I A

Here you can see two columns, the left one and the right one. You have to find which letter or number is in the left column but not in the right one, or vice versa. There may be one, two, or three elements that differ. In the first row, for example, the element that is missing in the left column is 3, and in the right column it is 4. You can circle those that do not have a match in the adjacent column. Let's get started with the exercise itself. Good luck!

	Left column	*Right column*
1	3 9 7 2 8	8 7 2 4 9
2	W L B P X	W P X I A
3	C 4 1 T E	4 E C T 8
4	9 8 3 5 4 6	6 9 2 3 8 4
5	R N B L U A	L B R U A G
6	9 S 2 1 8 7	8 9 I 2 M S
7	8 7 1 4 5 6 2	6 9 2 3 1 4 7
8	X J A W B F U D	V S X P J B D W

For younger children, this same exercise can be done with everyday images, as shown below. Which objects are repeated in both rectangles?

Left column	*Right column*

Exercise 6: Prize for the most attentive

Below is a list of everyday words. You must remember as many words and as much information as you can for 30 seconds; then you will have to answer some questions. In this exercise, we work on both attention and memory. Ready? Let's get started with the words.

BICYCLE
PIPE
SCANDAL
GAMES
VAN DOG
ALICANTE
VEHICLE
STORM
SCHOOL

Cover up the words you just memorized.

Once you have memorized everything you can, you must answer the following questions:

- How many words were there in total?
- Do you remember if any words contained the letter H?
- Were there any verbs among the words?
- Did the word "truck" appear?
- And the last question: Did we name any cities?

Exercise 7: Abracadabra

Now we are going to do a very simple task, but one that requires your full attention. You will see a series of letters. Every time you see an X preceded by an A, you must raise both hands and say "abracadabra." This time, we will do it visually, but you can also do it aurally (by reading the words to your child or student). Ready? Go ahead.

T	A	X	G
X	A	D	A
X	L	X	A
X	Z	Y	X
A	P	A	X

A	X	A	Q
X	R	A	C
A	X	S	J
A	X	B	A
X	R	A	X

Exercise 8: Letter salad

Take a close look at the following table. It has a lot of letters. We can only see the letters b, d, p, and q. The task is to color each rectangle with a color based on the letter. If you look closely, there is a legend below the letters that tells you what color each one should be. For example, the b's should be colored red, the d's blue, the p's yellow, and finally, the q's green. Based on this idea, you can create many other exercises to work on your children's or students' focused attention, always adapting them to their age and characteristics.

b	q	d	p	q	d	p	b	q	p
q	d	p	b	b	q	d	p	q	p
d	p	q	b	b	p	q	d	p	b
p	d	b	q	d	p	d	p	b	b
d	p	b	b	p	q	d	p	q	b
p	d	d	b	q	d	p	q	p	b
q	d	p	b	d	q	d	p	q	b
p	q	d	p	b	b	q	d	p	q
d	p	q	b	d	p	d	p	b	b
b	q	d	p	q	d	p	b	p	d

Red = b	Blue = d	Yellow = p	Green = q

Exercise 9: Orange juice

In the following table, there are enough oranges to make juice for an entire town. If you look closely, there are three oranges in each box, but one of them is different from the other two. Look carefully, you must pay close attention. Your task is to cross out the orange that is different from the other two in each of the forty boxes. Go ahead and make some delicious juice!

Exercise 10: Find and compare

To finish the topic, you must search among these two pairs of round cards for the object that is present in both cards. There is only one object that matches in both. Which one is it?

Chapter 6

Exercises to develop impulse control

Inhibiting impulses throughout history

Impulse control is one of the executive functions that most differentiates us from other animals, and it is also one of the last to be acquired by children. Since the dawn of humanity, there has been talk of controlling impulses and resisting temptation. It is even mentioned in the Bible. Adam and Eve are tempted by the serpent to eat the forbidden apple. Since they were unable to use their executive functions correctly—specifically, their ability to resist temptation—they were expelled from paradise. Today, we call this impulse control or, sometimes, inhibitory control or impulse inhibition.

Folk tales also provide numerous examples that highlight the importance of inhibitory control. For example, in the tale of *The Ant and the Grasshopper*, the grasshopper symbolizes emotional and instinctive control, while the ant represents the prefrontal cortex. There are also numerous quotes from famous people that refer to this executive function: Oscar Wilde said that "The only thing I can't resist is temptation," and the brilliant Groucho Marx said, "It is better to remain silent and be thought a fool than to open your mouth and remove all doubt." If you remember, in the car metaphor we presented in Chapter 2, we said that impulse control corresponded to the brakes on a car.

Now imagine the following situation. You have been allowed to ride a bicycle. It appears to be a normal bicycle, but when you ride it, you realize that it is special. Every time you want to turn right, you have to turn the handlebars to the left, and every time you want to turn left, you have to turn the handlebars in the opposite direction. It's like playing in a world turned upside down: you have to turn in the direction you don't want to go. This is inhibitory control: trying to control the information or automatic responses that we have established in a very unconscious and rigid way.

DOI: 10.4324/9781003794332-6

The Golosina test

One of the most representative studies of inhibitory control and its consequences is the famous marshmallow experiment. In the 1960s, Walter Mischel conducted a study at Stanford University (United States) to see how well preschool children could delay gratification and control their impulses to eat a marshmallow.

To do this, the researcher placed a treat, candy, or marshmallow in front of the child. The researcher told the child that they had to leave the room for a few minutes. The child could eat the treat at any time, but if they managed to wait until the researcher returned, they would receive double the reward. This is a classic exercise for testing reward delay. I encourage you to try it at home with your young (and not so young) children. One of the many conclusions of this study was that 5-year-olds have better executive functioning in inhibiting their impulses to eat the treat than 3- and 4-year-olds, meaning they are better able to delay gratification and wait. All of this is consistent with what we have been saying so far. The brain needs time and experience to acquire different executive functions. The candy test, also known as *the marshmallow test*, yielded many interesting conclusions. Those children who were able to wait for the researcher to return and thus obtained double the reward, when they reached adolescence:

- They scored higher on intelligence tests.
- They showed greater self-control in frustrating situations.
- They gave in less to temptation.
- They were less distracted when trying to concentrate.
- They were more self-confident.
- In stressful situations, they did not lose their cool as easily as those who could not resist the temptation to eat the candy.
- They were more forward-thinking and planned things more (better organizational skills).
- They were more persistent in their various tasks.
- They listened more to reason and were therefore more decisive.
- They scored much higher on academic aptitude tests.

In conclusion, we can say that these adolescents were the opposite of the stereotype of the troubled teenager. The children who ate the candy were more impulsive when they grew up than the children who resisted temptation, who were more thoughtful. Those who resisted had a more active prefrontal cortex years later, making it easier for them to solve problems, be creative, control their impulses, etc. On the other hand, the children who could not resist the temptation grew up to be kids who had a more active medial prefrontal cortex, which led them to engage in behaviors guided by desire and pleasure without considering what was desirable and reasonable. In addition, these children were more likely to develop an addiction.

What is impulse control?

We can define impulse control as the ability we have to control, stop, or postpone certain stimuli or actions that are not relevant to the task we are performing in the present moment. For example, it is important for a child to know how to inhibit the impulse to hit another child simply because they scored a goal.

The consequence of not having well-developed inhibitory processes is what we know as impulsivity. Children who are classified as impulsive, whether behaviorally or verbally, have difficulty controlling their impulses. For example, a significant percentage of children and adolescents with ADHD exhibit impulsivity. In younger children, impulsivity is usually motor-based, that is, observable, while in adolescents, it tends to be cognitive impulsivity, that is, unobservable, as it is related to thoughts.

Impulse inhibition is a key executive function in the society we live in. It is just as important to be able to perform certain behaviors as it is to be able to inhibit them. The example I like to use to explain this is the metaphor of the tightrope walker. In order to successfully maintain balance on the wire, it is important to coordinate both the actions you need to perform and the moments when you should not move forward. It is an action where inhibition takes on special importance. The main brain neurotransmitter involved in inhibitory processes is GABA, gamma-aminobutyric acid. People who have a good ability to regulate, control, or delay their impulses in most situations know, like the tightrope walker, when to move forward and when to stop and maintain their balance so as not to fall into the void.

Exercise 1: Animal Stroop

We begin with a classic activity known as the *Stroop* effect. You may not be familiar with the name, but once you do the activity, I'm sure it will ring a bell. Next, you will see some pictures of animals. Your task is to say what animals they are. Be careful because later on, when the name of an animal appears superimposed, it may be a little more difficult. The exercise has three parts in order of difficulty.

Task 1: Name the animals you see. The route is always from top to bottom and from left to right, that is, as we normally read.

Task 2: In this second task, you must also name the pictures of the animals you can see in the image below.

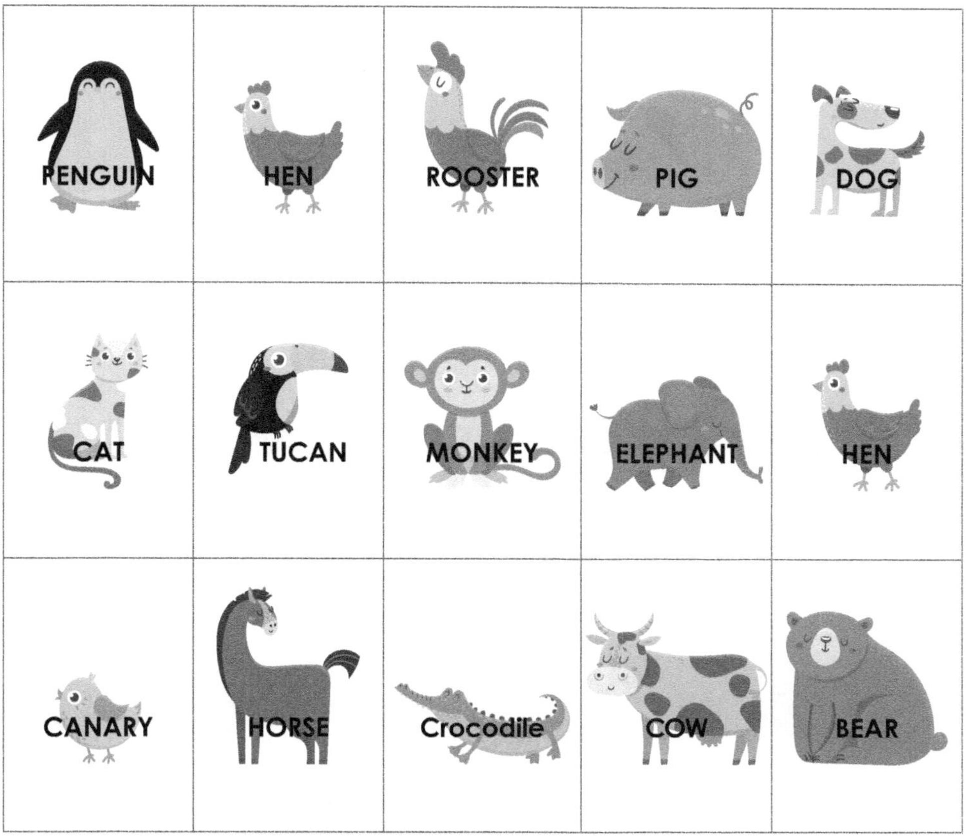

Task 3: Finally, let's move on to the most difficult task. You have to name the animal you see in each of the pictures.

Exercise 2: Everyone says yes

In this exercise, only two stimuli will appear: "Yes" or "Yes*." The only difference between the two words is the asterisk. When you see "Yes," you will say yes. But if you see "Yes*," you must inhibit that yes and say "No." Understood? Go ahead then.

Yes	Yes*	Yes*	Yes
Yes*	Yes*	Yes	Yes
Yes	Yes*	Yes*	Yes*
Yes	Yes*	Yes	Yes
Yes	Yes	Yes*	Yes
Yes*	Yes*	Yes	Yes*
Yes	Yes*	Yes	Yes*

Exercise 3: Detective González

Detective González has been assigned two tasks, one simpler and one somewhat more complicated In the first task, the detective has to circle all the objects he finds that are neither bicycles nor frogs. Will you help him?

The second task for which Detective Gonzalez needs your help is a little more complicated. Now you must circle all the objects you find that are not sunglasses, a water bottle, a basketball, or a dinosaur. Go ahead!

Exercise 4: Playing with numbers

In this exercise, the task is to count the total number of elements that appear in each rectangle. Both symbols and numbers may appear. However, if a thicker rectangle appears inside the rectangle, you should read the number that appears inside it. To understand this better, let's look at an example.

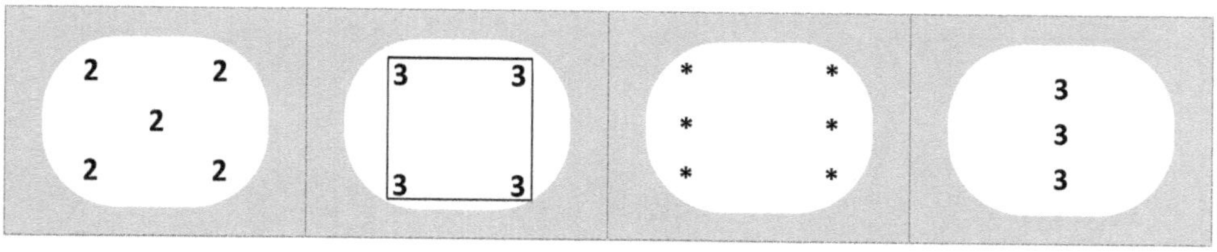

In the first rectangle, we would have to say five, since there are five elements. In the next one, since there is a thicker rectangle, we have to say three, since we have to read the number that appears repeatedly (and not the number of times that number appears). And in the next one? What would you say? The answer is six. And in the last one? The answer is three. Now that we've done the test questions, let's move on to the exercise itself.

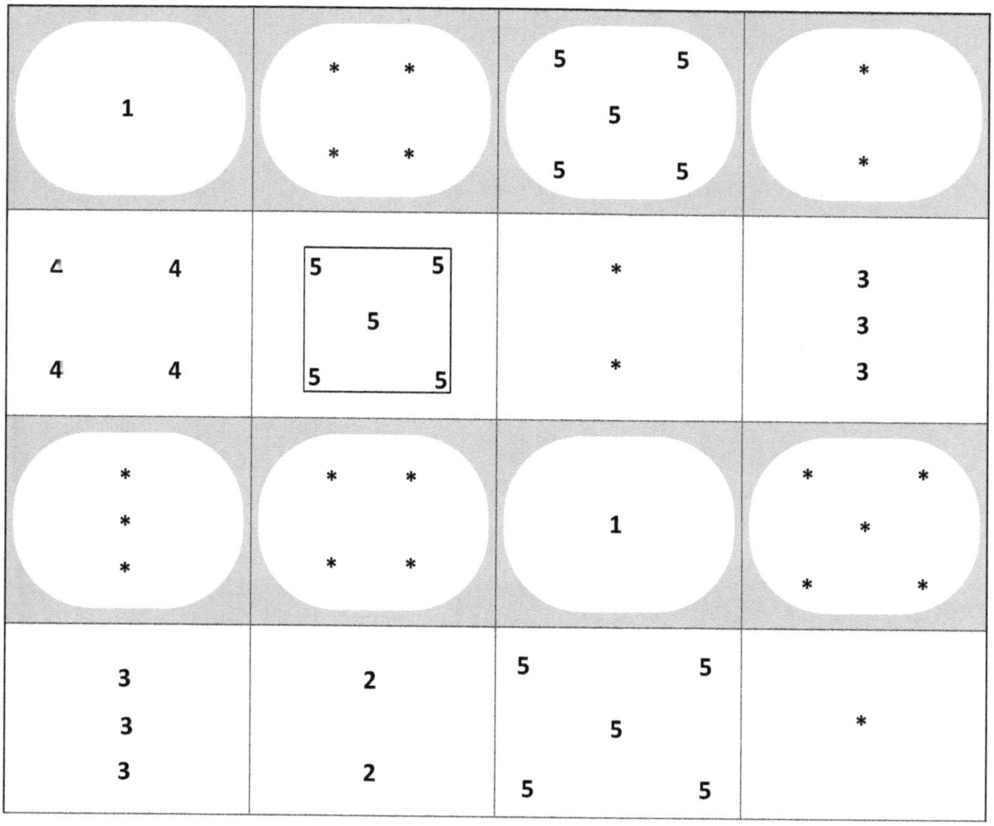

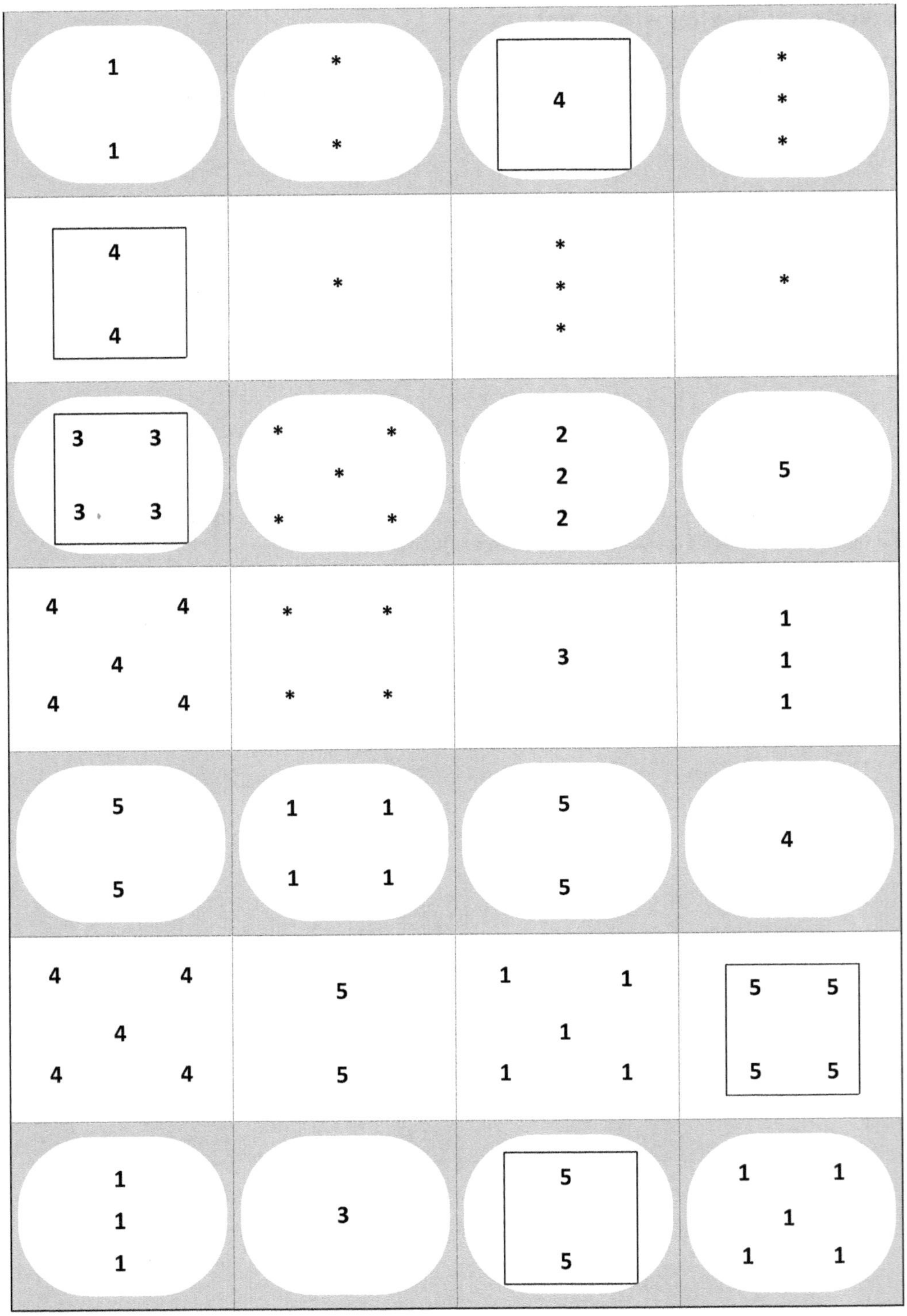
1 1
* *
4
* * *
4 4
*
* * *
*
3 3 3 3
* * * * *
2 2 2
5
4 4 4 4 4
* * * *
3
1 1 1
5 5
1 1 1 1
5 5
4
4 4 4 4 4
5 5
1 1 1 1 1
5 5 5 5
1 1 1
3
5 5
1 1 1 1 1

Exercise 5: One step forward

To do this exercise, you must stand up and have enough space to move around. You have to pay attention to the arrows you will see in the book. Whenever a black arrow appears, you must take a step in the direction it points. However, if the arrow is white, you should go in the opposite direction. In other words, if the arrow points up and is black, you take a step forward, but if it is white, you take a step backward. Let's try a few tests.

Since the arrow is black and points downwards, you have to take a step backward; the next one indicates a step to our left; and the third and last one in the training points upwards, but since it is white, we will take a step backward.

Okay? Let's begin!

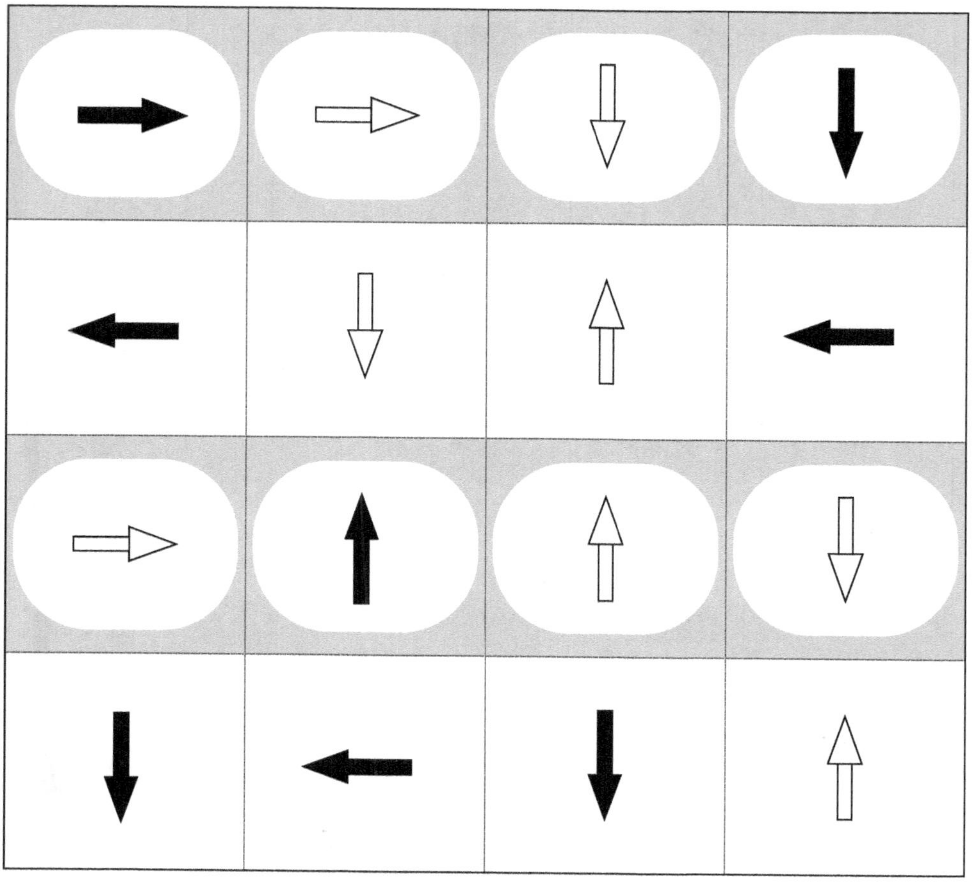

Exercise 6: A walk around the zoo

Let's imagine that this morning we visited the animals at the zoo. Below, you will see different animals that we can find at the zoo appear one by one. You should clap your hands every time an animal appears, but if you don't see an animal, you should refrain from clapping, OK? Let's get started.

Exercise 7: Sneakers and hands

Now we're going to do one of my favorite exercises. Every time you see a picture of clapping hands, you'll stamp your foot hard on the floor. When you see a picture of sneakers, you'll clap your hands. If you see other hand gestures, just copy them. Let's try a few.

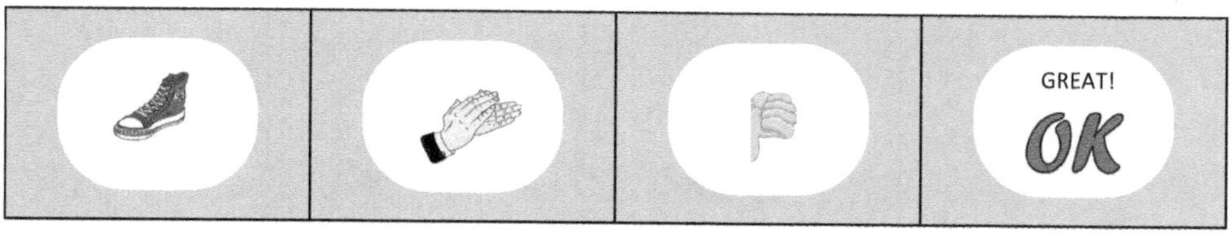

Perfect. You've seen how it works, right? Let's move on to the exercise itself.

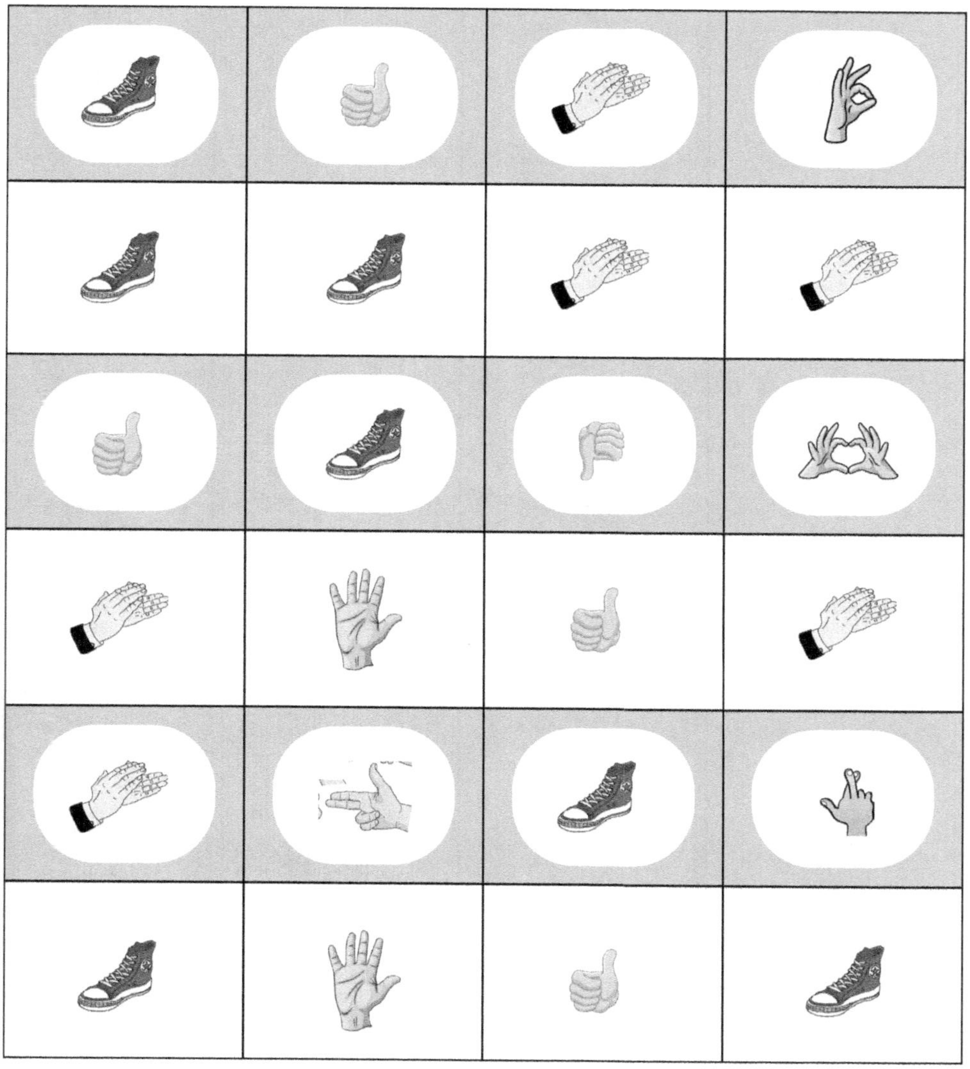

Exercise 8: Moon and sun

Now let's do an exercise aimed mainly at children in the early years of school. Every time you see a picture of the sun, say "moon," and when you see a moon, say "sun." Easy, right? Let's do it.

Every time the sun appears, you will say "moon," and when the moon appears, you will say nothing.

Exercise 9: Watch out for number 2!

Now you will see numbered billiard balls of different colors. But don't worry, because there are only two types. If you see a black ball with the number 2 in white, you will say 1, and when you see a white billiard ball with a black 2, you will say nothing. We will remain silent, okay? Let's go.

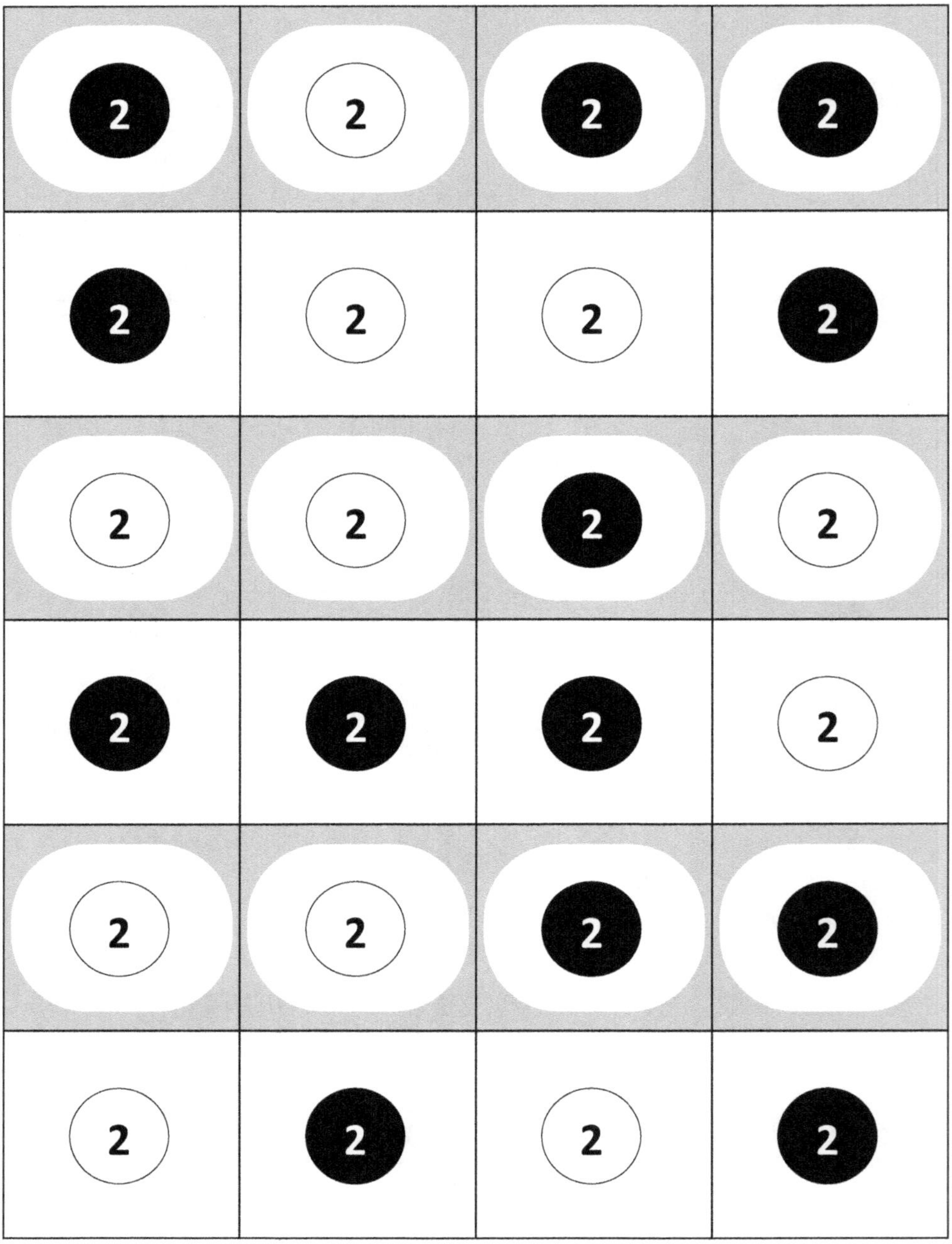

Exercise 10: The nosy windows

In the following, you will see a series of objects, all of which are familiar to you. Your task is to pay close attention because every time a picture of a door does not appear, you must say "window" loudly. When you see a picture of a door, you must remain silent. Go ahead!

Reference

Mischel, W., Ebbesen, E. B., & Raskoff Zeiss, A. (1972). Cognitive and attentional mechanisms in delay of gratification. *Journal of Personality and Social Psychology*, 21(2), 204–218. https://doi.org/10.1037/h0032198

Chapter 7

Exercises to develop working memory

What is working memory?

Working memory is our ability to retain, maintain, and manipulate a given piece of information. It is like an *online* memory. *Working* memory is sometimes also referred to as *working memory* because, as we said, its purpose is to work with certain information in the present moment. It is the memory we use to solve a problem. The keyword for working memory is "for," since this type of memory is used *to* solve something in the future, but taking the past into account. We could say that working memory is a necessary, but not sufficient, condition for decision-making. Therefore, it operates or manipulates the information that we are keeping *online or* in the present moment. Cerebrally speaking, working memory is located in the dorsolateral prefrontal cortex.

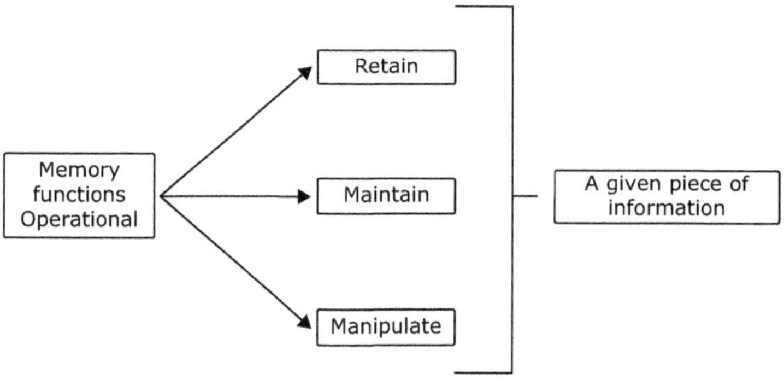

Traditional accounts of short-term memory often described its capacity as 7 ± 2 items, meaning that people can retain between 5 and 9 items on average. Working memory is therefore a limited system. For example, would you be able to solve the following mental calculation if, instead of being written down, it were given to you verbally?

$$5 - 3 + 8 - 7 + 1 - 3 + 9 + 5 + 2 - 4 + 7$$

Wouldn't that be very difficult? This is because our working memory is limited and cannot store such a large amount of information.

DOI: 10.4324/9781003794332-7

Working memory is a type of short-term memory (STM), but they are not synonymous. Working memory differs from STM in that the latter serves only to store data, while working memory, as we have already explained, uses that data to perform a mental operation. We are using our STM when we try to remember a car license plate number, a phone number, or a street address. In these two cases, there is no manipulation of information, only retention and maintenance. On the other hand, spelling the word COMPUTER backward involves activating and using our working memory, as we must store the information, perform an operation, and give a final result. This is what we metaphorically refer to as *online* memory.

One way to exercise a child's working memory is to count the number of coins or add up the amount of euros in our wallet. To give the correct answer, the child must add up each coin and update the result. Other ways to exercise working memory include mathematical calculations, spelling words backward, etc.

Types of memory

Memory is a psychological function that allows us to learn, retain information, and adapt to the environment in which we live. In this way, we can remember past experiences. Human memory, unlike animal memory—which acts mainly on the basis of their present needs—can contemplate the past and plan for the future. We use memory in everyday activities such as walking, riding a bike, remembering who the current president is, calculating 2 × 3 × 4, remembering what ingredients we need to make a recipe, or knowing our name and where our parents are from. In all these cases, we are using memory, but is there only one type of memory? If you look at the following diagram, you will see that there are four different types of memory, each with its own characteristics that make it special and unique:

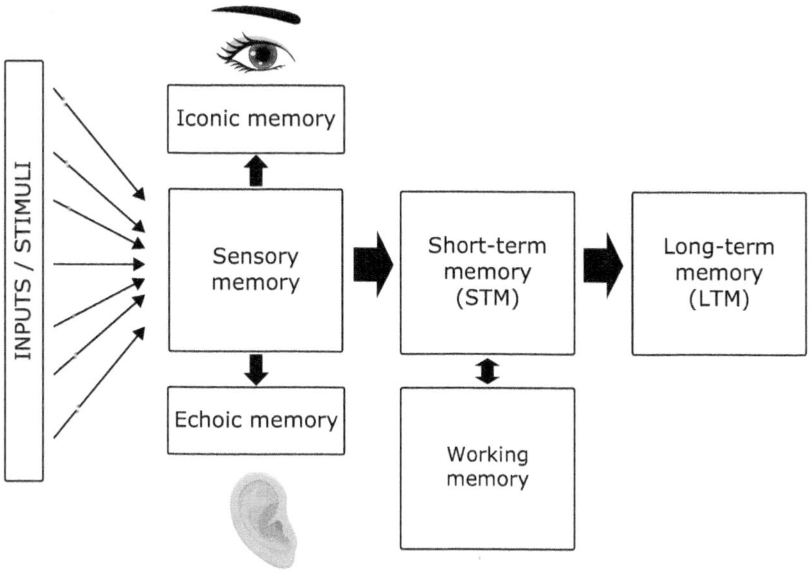

- **Sensory memory:** It is also known as sensory storage. We capture external information through the five senses (sight, hearing, touch, smell, and taste), and when it reaches the brain, neurons are responsible for recognizing or storing that information. There are a total of five sensory stores, one for each of the senses. The two most relevant in humans are *iconic memory* (sight) and *echoic memory* (hearing). In this type of memory, information is active for only milliseconds or, at most, a few seconds. After that time, if the person has not paid attention to the information, it will fade away.
- **Short-term memory (STM):** Here, information remains active for longer than in sensory memory. This information can remain in STM for quite some time through repetition; otherwise, it usually lasts about ten seconds. We must remember that STM has limited capacity.
- **Working memory:** Working memory is a type of STM but, unlike STM, it has the ability to manipulate or operate on information to produce a result or response. Working memory is divided into verbal and nonverbal, as we have the ability to operate with numbers as well as symbols, geometric figures, etc.
- **Long-term memory:** We refer to this storage when we talk about memory in general, and it has unlimited capacity. Even so, there is a brain law that says that *what is not used is lost*. Therefore, even though the capacity of long-term memory is unlimited, if the material is not used regularly, it tends to disappear.

We can also classify memory as implicit or explicit depending on the type of material stored:

- **Explicit or declarative memory:** We are aware of the information stored in this type of memory and can therefore explain it in words (give a narrative).

  It is not until the age of 2–3 that explicit memory begins to develop because until then, we have been functioning with procedural memories. The areas of the brain that are activated by explicit or declarative memory are the hippocampus and the prefrontal cortex, among other structures.
- **Implicit or procedural memory:** This is a type of unconscious memory based on procedures such as riding a bike, tying shoelaces, or writing. Humans have and remember sensations from a very young age, but we find it very difficult to put them into words.

  This type of memory is not located in the prefrontal cortex, but is stored in the reptilian brain, specifically in the cerebellum, which is closely related to movement, balance, coordination of both fine and gross motor skills, etc.

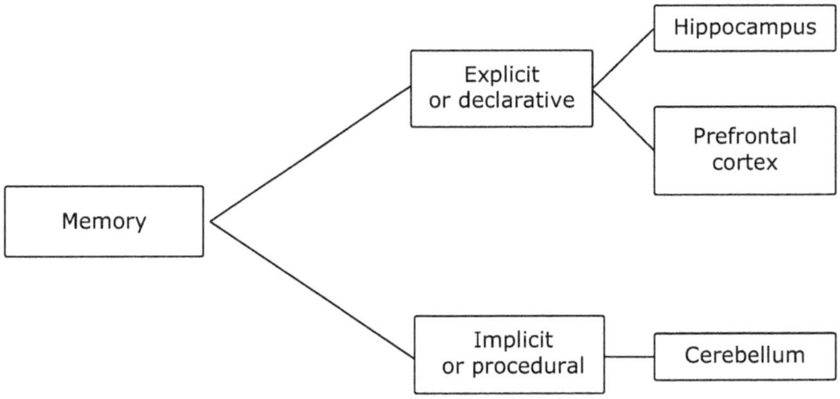

In this chapter, we will focus on developing exercises to promote and enhance working memory, since it is a type of executive memory and, therefore, is located in the prefrontal cortex.

Exercise 1: Number dance

Look closely at the number inside the rectangle below. Using this number, you must make the numbers dance in such a way that the following conditions are met.

92734

- Form the lowest number.
- Form three even numbers.
- Form the highest possible number.
- Form all possible five-digit numbers that start with three and end with nine.

Exercise 2: Nicolás the crab

This is an exercise in which the adult reads a series of numbers to the child or teenager, who must memorize them and then repeat them in reverse order. For example, if we say 2–6, they will have to say 6–2. Gradually increase the level of difficulty as they get better at it. The pace for reading the numbers is approximately one number per second.

2 elements:	5-7 / 4-1
3 elements:	5-1-8 / 9-3-6
4 elements:	3-7-1-8 / 5-9-2-6
5 elements:	4-2-8-5-9 / 9-4-6-1-2
6 elements:	6-2-4-8-1-9 / 3-4-1-6-5-9

Exercise 3: Counting euros

I am going to introduce you to six boys and girls who carry a coin purse in their pocket. As you can see in the following, each of them has taken all the money they have out of their coin purse. Your task is to count how many euros each of them has.

Ready? Go ahead.

 Laura		 Luis	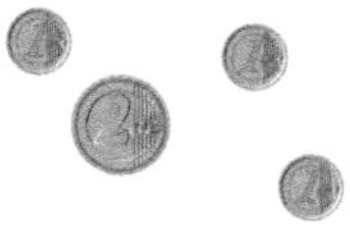

 Julia		 Miguel	
 Susana		 Jonás	

Exercise 4: The human calculator

In the following, you will find a series of questions that you must answer:

a How much is 60% of 10?
b Which is greater, 10% of 50 or 50% of 10?
c How many legs do 32 horses have?
d How many times do the hands of an analog clock cross each other in a day?
e How many seconds are there in 17 and a half minutes?
f How many days are there in total in the months of May, January, March, and September?
g What is the square root of 144?
h How many eyes do seven one-eyed pirates have?

Exercise 5: Sudoku

Solve the following two Sudoku puzzles. The first one is easier and the second one is a little more complex. Go ahead.

			3
3		4	2
2		3	1

	3					4	7	
		4		7				8
8	7		6		4			2
		5			8	2		6
3		2	4			7		5
				2	7			3
5	4		9	6		3	8	
				4	3		6	
							2	

Exercise 6: King Kong

Below, you will see a series of numbers. You must bang on the table King Kong style every time you see a number that is double the previous one. Let's do this. Warm up your fists!

6	10	5	10
18	1	2	4
9	7	16	8
16	3	6	12
1	3	5	11
4	8	3	6

Exercise 7: Crazy numbers

Take a close look at the following exercise. It consists of filling in the boxes with numbers and mathematical symbols so that all the columns and rows are correct.

10	+	3	=	
		-		-
	+	1	=	3
=		=		=
	+	2	=	

	-	3	=	
+		+		+
6	-		=	2
=		=		=
	-	7	=	7

10		14	=	24
-		-		
2	+		=	15
=		=		=
	+		=	9

26	-	17	=	
+				+
	-	5	=	2
=		=		=
33		22	=	

Exercise 8: Thinking about numbers

This activity is simple, but it requires a lot of concentration, as we must always follow the same pattern. We will start with a given number. We will add 2 and subtract 3. So, for example, if the number we are given is 34, we first add 2, giving us 36, and then we subtract 3, giving us 33, and so on until we reach zero. OK? Depending on the child's age, we will give them more or fewer operations and start with one number or another. In this case, following the same formula as before (adding 2 and subtracting 3), we will start with the number 15 so as not to make it too long. Go ahead.

Exercise 9: Card memory

For this activity, we will need a Spanish deck of cards. The more cards we use, the more difficult the game will be. The activity consists of placing all the cards face down and turning over only two at a time; if they form a pair, they will remain face up; if not, we will turn them back over. The pair can be formed by having the same number or the same suit. The goal is to remember where the cards are positioned in order to form pairs.

Exercise 10: Use your mental dictionary

For this last exercise, you will need to concentrate hard and memorize all the words that are read to you. Your task is to remember the words we say and then put them in alphabetical order, as if it were a dictionary. As you do well, we will include a few more words. Keep in mind that if the child or teenager cannot see the words because we are saying them aloud, the exercise is much more difficult than if they can see them.

Game	Colony				
Horse	Wardrobe				
Room	Frog	Tomato			
Eggplant	Heat	Humidity			
Case	Hair	Computer	Water		
Racket	Ski	Basketball	Ball	Basketball	
Pipe	Oven	Mallow	Pen	Goal	Pencils

Chapter 8

Exercises to develop cognitive flexibility

What is cognitive flexibility?

Cognitive flexibility is our ability to generate different hypotheses or attempts when solving a specific problem; that is, our ability to come up with many hypotheses for the same situation or problem. One of the psychological functions most closely related to cognitive flexibility is creativity. Creative people are very flexible, which is why they come up with so many exceptional ideas. Therefore, cognitive flexibility is the opposite of cognitive rigidity.

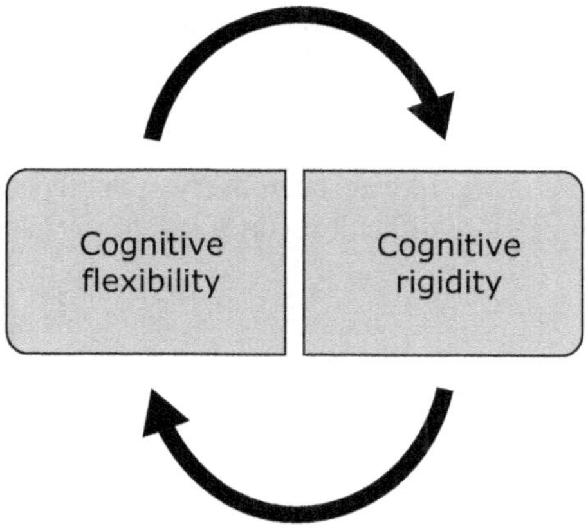

Yes, but what are the differences between flexible and rigid people, cognitively speaking? Obsessive, narcissistic, and impulsive people tend to have a rigid cognitive pattern, as they only accept one way of solving problems. It is difficult for them to find alternatives to a problematic situation. Let's look at these three examples in more detail. The obsessive person needs to turn the light switch on and off several times to feel calm. For a narcissist to feel good, others must speak well of them; otherwise, they will not feel good or will blame others for not appreciating them. And finally, the impulsive person does not know how to act differently. They are rigid because they always react in the same way. In contrast, a child with cognitive flexibility will consider and evaluate different options before making a decision.

DOI: 10.4324/9781003794332-8

A task that requires good cognitive flexibility would be one in which we have to change activities every so often and adapt to the changing characteristics of each exercise. Imagine that we are riding in a virtual reality car with pedals. We are going on a journey and must use the accelerator and brake pedals to move forward and stay on the road. But after driving for a minute, a siren sounds and the pedals' functions reverse: the one that used to brake now accelerates, and the one that used to accelerate now brakes. How would you adapt to this change? This would be an exercise in cognitive flexibility. Depending on how flexible or rigid we are cognitively, we will perform better or worse in this type of test. It will be easier or more difficult for us to adapt to changing circumstances in the environment.

Exercise 1: Pull everything you can think of out of a hat

Think for a minute about all the things we could do with the following items:

- A brick
- A strainer
- A mirror
- A golf ball
- A picture frame

Exercise 2: The matchstick bull

Chopstick-based activities can be useful for developing and strengthening cognitive flexibility. These exercises are usually very popular with children and teenagers. Below, you will see a bull made with chopsticks facing to the left. Your task is to make it face to the right with only three movements of the chopsticks. You can move any three chopsticks to make the bull face in the opposite direction. Remember that the bull must end up with the same characteristics it had at the beginning: two front legs, two hind legs, two horns, and a tail. Now try to solve the challenge.

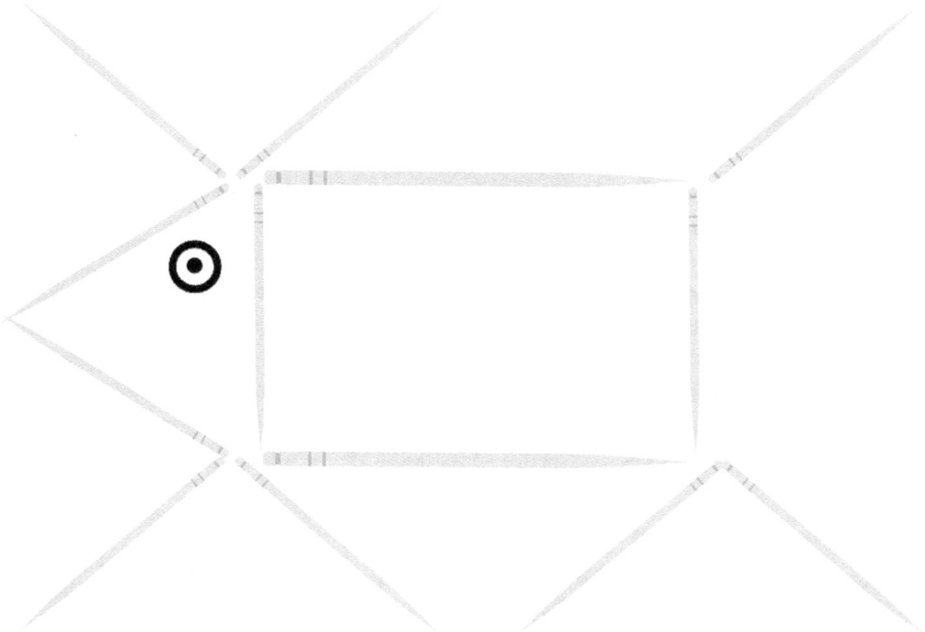

Exercise 3: The magic triangle

As you can see below, there is a triangle made with tennis balls. The objective is to make the vertex that points upward end up pointing downward with only three ball movements. Of course, it is essential that the shape remain a triangle. If you find it difficult to visualize it this way, you can build the triangle using small paper balls.

Exercise 4: The five dots

As you can see, there is a square with five dots at the bottom. Does it not resemble the number five on a die? Your task is to be as creative as possible: you must draw as many different shapes as you can think of on the sheet below. You can connect as many dots as you like with straight lines. The important thing is that you do not repeat any shapes.

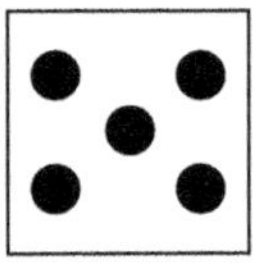

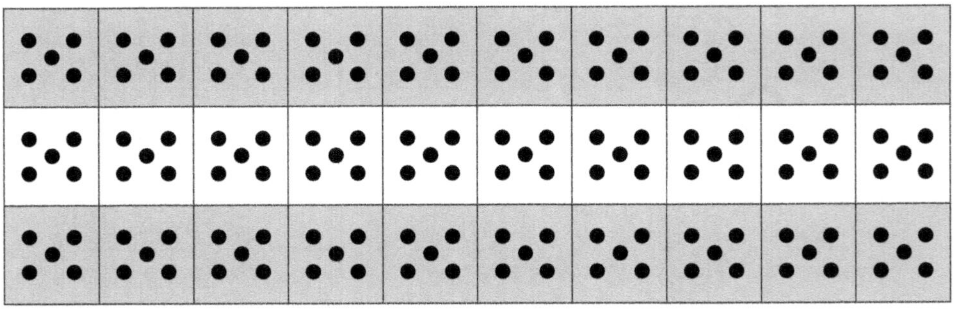

Exercise 5: Matchsticks and numbers

Below, you will see a number made with chopsticks. The number is 5986. You must make the number as large as possible with only two movements of the chopsticks. Try to solve the challenge? You can place the chopsticks wherever you want, but only two chopsticks can be moved.

Exercise 6: All the words

Your task is to name all the words you can think of that begin with, contain, or end with a given letter or syllable. We will adapt these instructions depending on the age and level of the child.

For example, for young children, we can ask them to name all the words that begin with the letter D. If we want to make it more difficult, we can ask them to name words that begin with the letter T and end in a vowel. More complex examples of this exercise would be four-syllable words that end in TA and include any other vowel. Another complex example would be words that have an M or an N and contain at least two vowels. As you can see, depending on the age of the child, we adapt the instructions, but we work on cognitive flexibility in the same way. Use your imagination to create new variations.

Exercise 7: Four straight lines

Next, we are going to play one of my favorite games for working on cognitive flexibility, among other executive functions, because we also work on concentration, anticipation, planning, decision-making, etc. As you can see below, we have a square made up of nine dots. The objective of the game is to connect those nine dots without lifting the pencil from the paper and using only four straight lines. Ready? Begin.

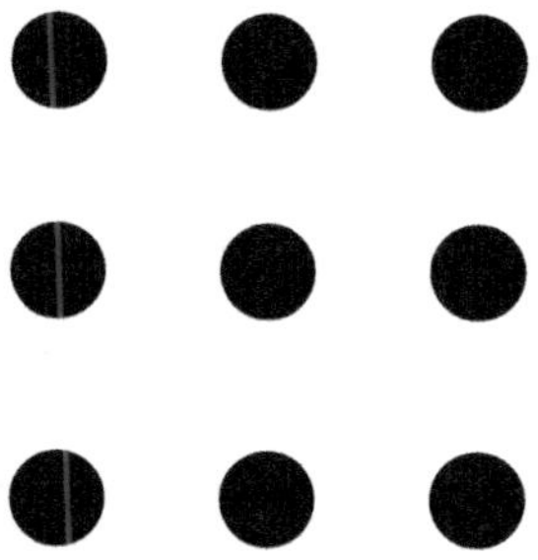

Exercise 8: Addition and subtraction

As you can see in the following table, left-hand column contains additions, and the right-hand column contains subtractions. Your task is to start by adding and, after 15 seconds, switch to the right-hand column and start subtracting. The table can be as long and complex as you like, depending on the child or teenager you are working with.

Additions	*Subtractions*
6 + 13	17−12
16 + 26	23−3−4
7 + 3 + 19	42−17
23 + 12	34−21
3 + 4 + 7	54−27
11 + 18 + 23	14−3−5
4 + 56 + 21	34−13
19 + 23	32−21−3
45 + 23	45−32
65 + 21 + 34	11−7−1
66 + 21 + 2	65−3−22

Exercise 9: Finding Nemo

Nemo is lost at sea. Can you get him to change direction? Instead of going left, you must help him change direction to the right, but only with three movements of the chopsticks.

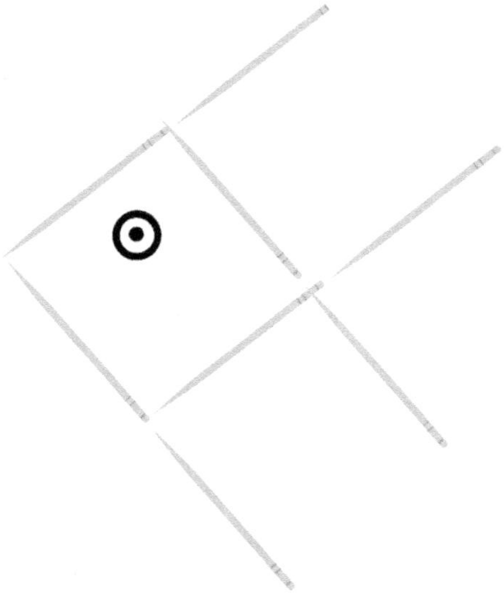

Exercise 10: Picasso's abstraction

This exercise for working on cognitive flexibility consists of asking the child to draw as many designs as possible on a sheet of paper using six straight lines in one minute. The lines can be of different lengths, but there must always be six, no more and no fewer. Then, to increase the level of difficulty, ask them how many different designs they can create using two circles and a square? They have one minute to complete the task.

Chapter 9

Exercises to develop planning skills

What is planning?

Planning or organization comes into play when we visualize the different ways we can solve a particular problem. Therefore, planning comes into play before implementing the chosen option or alternative. We could say that it is the prelude to decision-making.

For example, imagine that you leave work and head home. You get in your car and set off for home using your usual route. When you are only five minutes away from your destination, you find that there are roadworks on that street. At that moment, your executive functioning kicks in so that you can plan the best options for getting from that point to your home. We organize ourselves, visualize the different options, and make the decision we believe to be most effective.

One way we can help children practice planning is by creating mazes of varying difficulty depending on the child's characteristics and age.

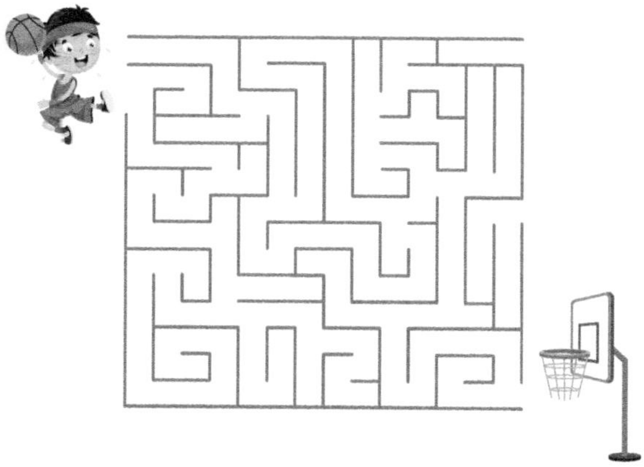

DOI: 10.4324/9781003794332-9

Exercise 1: What a mess!

Below, you can see a series of vignettes that are out of order. Your task is to arrange them in such a way that they make sense.

Exercise 2: Tower of Hanoi

One of the classic ways to work on planning and organization is to build the Tower of Hanoi. The child's task is to move the discs of different sizes from the rod on the left to the rod on the right, but under a series of conditions. There are many websites where we can perform this exercise.

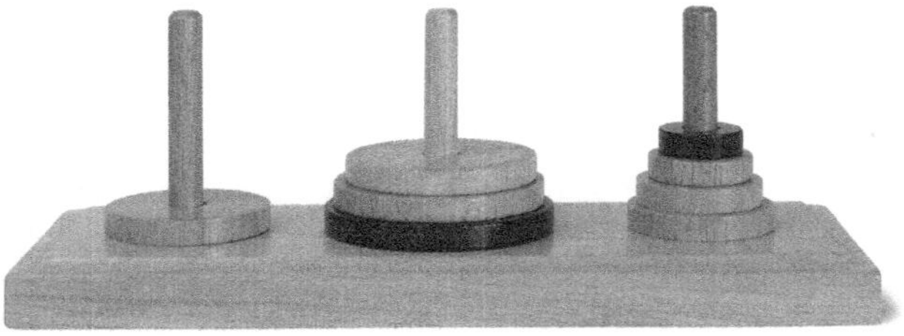

The four conditions that must be met to complete the Tower of Hanoi are as follows:

1 The discs can only be moved one at a time.
2 A large disc can never be placed on top of a smaller one.
3 Only the top disc on each rod can be moved.
4 You can use the middle rod to move all the discs to the right rod.

The good thing about the Tower of Hanoi is that it can be easily adapted. Here, it is suggested adapting it using coins. You can take as many coins of different sizes as you like, bearing in mind that the more coins you use, the more complex the game will be. Cut out three paper circles to use as the bases on which to place the coins, and begin the activity.

Exercise 3: Crazy numbers

Below, you will see a series of numbers in random order. Your task is to arrange all the numbers in ascending order, that is, from smallest to largest.

12 8

1

7

5

10 3

40

6 32

9

If you would like an additional challenge, here is another series, but this one is more complex.

3 13

33 12

8

25 1 14

10

5 21

2

24 7

If we previously did this in ascending order, we will now do it in descending order, that is, from highest to lowest.

14 17

3 55 87

45

22 4 9

0 33

Exercise 4: The French omelet

Below, you will see a series of steps on how to make a fantastic French omelet. The problem is that the cook has mixed up the steps, so you must put them in the correct order.

- Beat the eggs.
- Heat the oil.
- Flip the omelet.
- Serve the omelet on a plate.
- Add a pinch of salt.
- Crack the eggs.
- Hold the eggs.
- Pour the eggs into the pan.

Exercise 5: Mazes

A classic way to work on planning is through mazes. Depending on the age and characteristics of the child, we can propose simpler or more complex mazes. Try to solve the following mazes that we propose.

Exercise 6: Connecting the dots

Next, ycu must connect the following circles with numbers, starting with number 1 and ending with number 25.

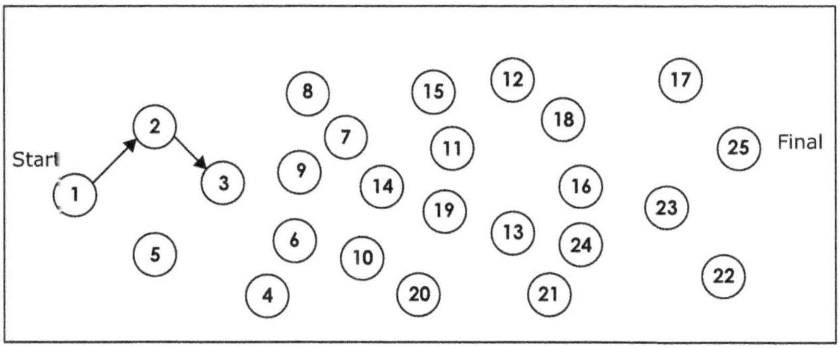

If you found this exercise easy or want a more complex task, try the next one. Now you will have to alternate numbers and letters, as you can see in the first example, which has already been completed.

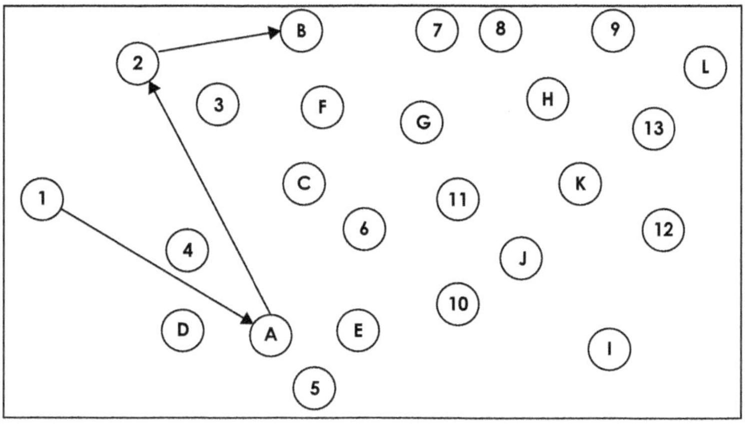

Exercise 7: Cats and dogs

Another classic game that helps develop planning skills is cats and dogs. We have three cats and three dogs on one side of the riverbank. The goal is to get them all to the other side using the boat, but there are two limitations:

- The boat has a maximum capacity of two animals.
- There cannot be more dogs than cats on either shore, as the dogs would eat the cats.

Exercise 8: The crazy dictionary

Below, you will see a series of everyday words. Your task is to classify them into one of the following three groups: tools, foods, and animals.

chickpeas wrench lion nail
strawberries ant hake bear
screwdriver eggs
dog drill
bread beans
pliers hammer nut screw turbot

Tools	Food	Animals

Exercise 9: Number tutti-frutti

Look at the numbers in the following image. Try to remember as much information as you can for 30 seconds, because then you will have to answer some questions.

32				13	
			23		
	5	9			
41				1	
12			89		57

Now, answer the following questions:

- Name all the even numbers.
- Order the odd numbers from smallest to largest.
- Order the even numbers from largest to smallest.
- Order the numbers greater than 10 and less than 50 from smallest to largest.

If you find this exercise too difficult or too easy, you can modify it to suit your level.

Exercise 10: The king of symbols

Look closely at the symbols associated with each of the numbers from 1 to 15. You will see that there are different symbols, although some are very similar. Your task is to draw the symbol corresponding to each number that appears in the following table. This exercise requires concentration, good planning, and perseverance. Try to complete it!

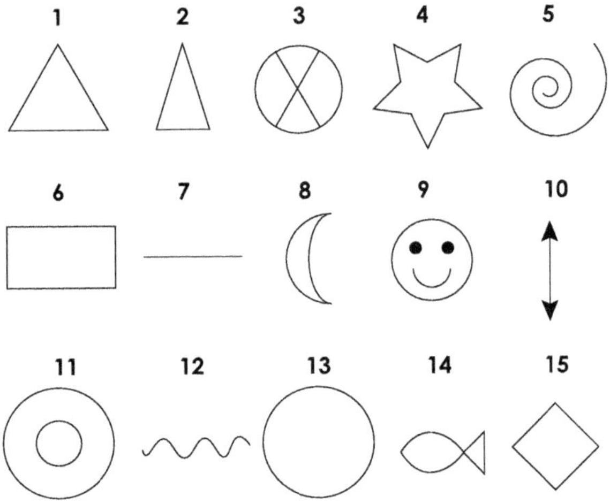

3	4	15	10	1	2	7	12	5	9	4
1	2	15	12	10	1	4	5	8	3	3
5	2	1	15	9	5	7	3	2	1	12
5	14	7	4	2	9	4	12	11	10	8
2	6	5	12	14	2	14	1	12	6	7
3	8	10	11	15	8	7	4	12	1	13
10	3	6	7	13	1	10	12	4	15	7
11	9	5	11	7	5	13	12	5	10	8
13	12	4	12	7	3	9	14	5	11	1

Chapter 10

Exercises to develop problem-solving skills

What is problem-solving?

Problem-solving involves the prefrontal cortex activating a series of attentional, memory, and motivational resources, among others, to search for different possible solutions to a given problem and make the decisions we consider most correct.

As you can see, problem-solving requires coordination with other executive functions and also involves other more emotional and motivational variables (emotional brain). It is clear that we will be more persistent and successful if we are motivated. In order to solve a problem in an appropriate and adapted way, children and adolescents will need to go through a series of stages consciously and voluntarily, which requires time, motivation, and perseverance. First, the child must be able to identify the problem, understand the objective they have been given, list the different options for solving it, choose a solution, implement it, and evaluate whether the decision they have made is successful or not. If not, they must implement other options they had already considered or even some new ones.

DOI: 10.4324/9781003794332-10

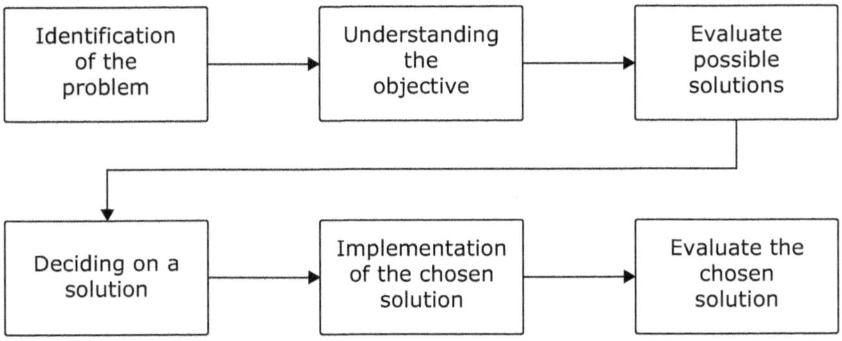

Problem-solving, sometimes also referred to as problem resolution, has a lot to do with cognitive flexibility, as a certain amount of flexibility and openness is necessary to be able to solve different problems. Children who are cognitively rigid, such as those diagnosed with ADHD, will have more difficulty effectively resolving these conflicts or problems.

Below, as we have done in previous chapters, we present a series of problems in the form of games or riddles for you to propose to your children or students. I hope you enjoy them as much as I do.

Exercise 1: The little house

This first exercise consists of drawing a little house like the one shown below. There are only two rules: you cannot lift your pencil from the paper, and you cannot go over the same spot twice. Let's see how many attempts it takes you to complete it. Good luck!

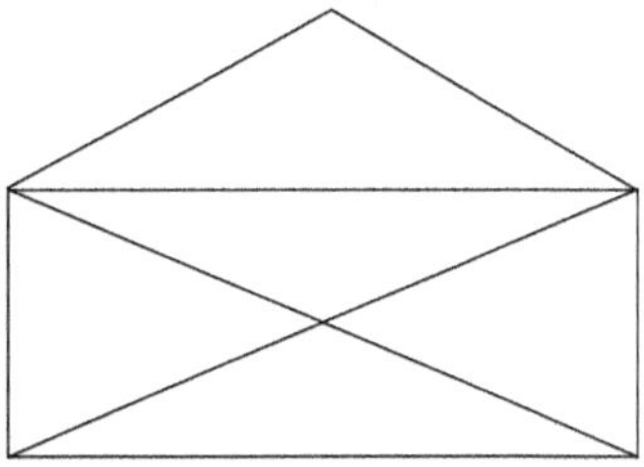

Exercise 2: Hunting mice

If 5 cats catch 5 mice in 5 minutes, how many cats will catch 100 mice in 100 minutes?

Exercise 3: The hourglasses

We have two hourglasses. One of them lasts 7 minutes, and the other 11 minutes. We know that rice takes 15 minutes to cook. If we leave it for less time, the rice will be hard, and if we leave it for more than 15 minutes, the rice will be overcooked. How can we know exactly when 15 minutes have passed with these two hourglasses? Specify the steps you will follow to ensure that the rice is cooked to perfection.

11 minutes 7 minutes

Exercise 4: Nineland

Nineland is a very special place. It has coins worth 1, 9, 99, and 999 florins. What is the smallest number of coins needed to pay exactly 6351 florins? What type of coins are they? Ready? Let's go for it.

Exercise 5: The ages

Juan is five years older than his brother Antonio and Francisco is as old as Juan and Antonio combined. Between the three of them, they add up to a total of 70 years. Can you tell me how old each one is?

Exercise 6: The candy boxes

As you can see in the image, we have three opaque boxes filled with candies. The boxes are labeled with the following names: mint, anise, and the mixture of mint and anise. The problem is that none of the labels are on the correct box. Can you find out how many candies we must remove and from which boxes in order to place the three labels correctly?

Exercise 7: The chocolate cups

Three children have to divide 21 cups among themselves, 7 of which are completely full of chocolate, another 7 are half full of chocolate, and 7 are empty. Can they divide the cups and chocolate so that each child gets the same amount of chocolate and the same number of cups? It is important to note that it is forbidden to transfer chocolate from one cup to another.

Exercise 8: Letter addition

As you can see below, we have a set of letters. Each letter corresponds to a number between zero and nine. Your mission is to guess which number each letter corresponds to. Numbers cannot be repeated. In total, there are ten different letters for ten numbers ranging from zero to nine. The only clue given at the beginning is that T = 0. This is a very interesting and motivating exercise for students in the last years of elementary school and the first years of middle school. It will probably take them several attempts.

DONALD
+ GERALD

ROBERT

Exercise 9: The water fountain

Imagine you are standing in front of a water fountain. How can you fill a container with 4 liters of water if you only have a 3-liter container and a 5-liter container?

Exercise 10: Curious Jonás

You must help Jonás identify the domino tile that should appear at the end of each of the three rows. Go ahead!

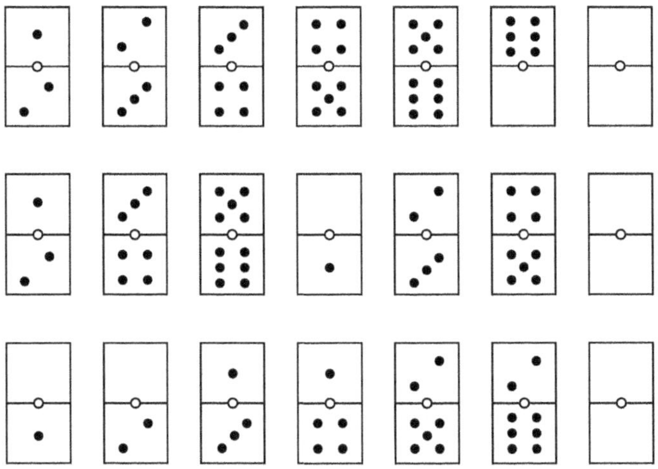

Chapter 11

Exercises to develop emotional self-regulation

What is emotional self-regulation?

Daniel Goleman, one of the world's leading experts on emotional education, defined emotional self-regulation as our ability to control our states, impulses, and internal resources. In other words, a child with good emotional self-regulation skills is one who knows how to identify their emotions and impulses and is able not to get to carried away by them when the situation does not call for it.

The metaphor of the carriage

Imagine for a moment that you are looking at a carriage pulled by a horse and driven by a coachman. The horse symbolizes momentum, energy, and strength, while the coachman symbolizes sanity, reflection, and thought. We could say that the carriage is the life of the person in question.

DOI: 10.4324/9781003794332-11

The horse represents the reptilian and emotional brain, while the carriage embodies, neuroanatomically speaking, the rational and executive brain. Both are essential for reaching your destination correctly. We need the strength of the horse and, in addition, the planning and execution skills of the coachman. Without a coachman, the horse would move aimlessly, and without a horse, the coachman would not be able to move that large, heavy carriage. Thus, both the horse (impulse and emotion) and the coachman (reason and execution) are essential for reaching the chosen destination. What's more, both are "condemned" to coordinate with each other. We can say that for there to be proper self-regulation of emotions in children or adolescents, it is essential that their coachman and horse be in tune and balanced.

What happens when our child or student is very angry? What if we are the ones who are angry? The mechanism is very similar in both children and adults.

When we experience a very intense emotion, like the child you see in the drawing, there is excessive activation of the emotional brain and inhibition of the executive brain (prefrontal cortex). For this reason, in such situations, we are much more emotional and impulsive than rational. It is as if the horse took control of the carriage while the coachman fell asleep. This phenomenon is known as *amygdala hijacking,* since it is this part of the brain that takes control of a person's life (carriage). What we have described occurs in both children and adults. The only difference is that adults have a greater capacity to manage emotions from the prefrontal cortex and also have more resources for emotional self-regulation than children.

How can we teach our children and students emotional self-regulation?

It is important to know that, since emotional self-regulation is something that is learned and not entirely genetically inherited, it is we adults who must teach our children and students to self-regulate. There are three steps that must be followed in the following order:

1 First, it is the adult (parent or teacher) who must have a good awareness and management of their emotions and impulses. This is what is known as emotional self-regulation on the part of the adult.
2 Second, adults heteroregulate children whenever they experience emotional conflict. Since children are not born knowing how to control or regulate themselves emotionally, it is adults who

must teach them strategies to do so. Children who are sad because they are not allowed to play soccer or angry because they failed a test need a significant adult to heteroregulate them. At this stage, the child is still dependent and needs the adult to help them find calm and balance.

3 Thanks to the experience and strategies that adults have provided over time, at this stage children are already capable of emotional self-regulation and can resolve emotional conflicts on their own. This does not mean that children are capable of resolving all emotional conflicts, but they do have strategies and tools that they can use.

The goal of emotional self-regulation is to adapt to the environment in the best way possible. For example, a child who habitually hits others in the playground to get what they want is not adapting to social norms. To this end, it is important for adults (parents, educators, psychologists, etc.) to teach children strategies so that they can gradually regulate themselves and their behavior becomes more adaptive than it currently is. In addition to emotional education provided by adults, it is important to note that the child's brain development is necessary, although not sufficient. Therefore, proper emotional development requires both education and adequate brain development.

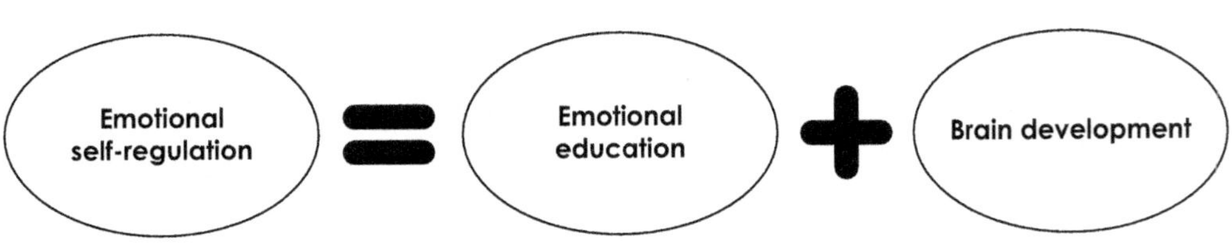

In the following, we will look at a series of exercises that help children and adolescents to better manage and control their impulses and emotions. As with the other executive functions we have already seen, some exercises are very simple because they are aimed at young children, while others are for older children. We must choose or adapt each exercise according to our needs.

Exercise 1: Looking it up in the dictionary

For this first exercise, you will need a dictionary. Look up the meaning of each emotion in the dictionary and give an example of each of the following basic emotions. If you already know the emotions and want to come up with your own definition, you can do so, although I recommend that you then look them up in the dictionary to check.

- Definition of **JOY**:
  → Give an example of a situation in which you felt happy:
- Definition of **SADNESS**:
  → Give an example of a situation in which you felt sad:
- Definition of **ANGER**:
  → Give an example of a situation in which you felt angry:
- Definition of **FEAR**:
  → Give an example of a situation in which you felt fear:
- Definition of **JEALOUSY**:
  → Give an example of a situation in which you have felt jealous:
- Definition of **BOREDOM**:
  → Give an example of a situation in which you felt bored:

Exercise 2: Breathing

Breathing exercises are very useful for our students and children when they are very emotionally activated. They are very effective in situations of anger, stress, or anxiety. There are many exercises for working on breathing. We will consider one simple exercise and divide it into four easy steps:

1 Breathe in deeply while counting to four in your head.
2 Hold your breath while counting mentally to four.
3 Exhale while counting mentally to eight.
4 Hold your breath for a couple of seconds and start the process again.

Exercise 3: Tension-release relaxation

Relaxation techniques are often linked to breathing techniques. Here, we will look at a very simple relaxation strategy developed by Jacobson called *tension relaxation*. The goal is to tense your muscles until they are tired. It is very useful in stressful situations, although I recommend practicing regularly so that the results are more noticeable and long-lasting. It can be done sitting down, although it is better to do it lying down, whenever possible. Since I am going to guide the relaxation exercise for children aged 5–7, we will work on large muscle groups to make it easier: arms and legs. The steps are given in the following:

1 We will start with the arms. We must stretch our arms and tense them as much as we can. We will hold this position for approximately ten seconds. When we release, we will pay attention to the feeling of relaxation and tranquility. We will perform this cycle with both arms at the same time and for three sets.
2 We continue with the legs. We stretch our legs and tense them as hard as we can, so that we feel and are aware of the tension they accumulate. After ten seconds, we stop tensing and notice the relaxation in our legs. Repeat the cycle three times.

Exercise 4: Sally and Ann

Theory of mind is our ability to understand that others may have a different point of view from our own. They may think and believe differently. This ability is acquired around the age of 4–5. The best way to check whether our child or student has theory of mind is to recreate the study on Sally and Ann, which you can see below. This activity can be acted out as if it were a play. Theory of mind is closely related to empathy.

Drawing by Sergio Cordero Cañizares

Exercise 5: Can you hold out?

This is one of my favorite exercises for working on emotional self-regulation, especially in cases of children and adolescents who get bored easily. It consists of sitting for five minutes on a chair or sofa without any kind of stimulation. In other words, you can't talk to anyone, look at your cell phone, listen to music, watch TV, etc. All you have to do is sit there for five minutes without doing anything. It's a good test to see how well you can tolerate boredom. In a society as hyperactive as ours, doing this is extremely difficult. It's an exercise I suggest to many of my patients, and I can tell you that a high percentage of them are unable to do it and end up giving up. With younger children, we can ask them to sit for two to three minutes, depending on their age and difficulties.

Exercise 6: The calm corner

It is important for children to have resources and strategies whenever a situation or emotion overwhelms them. Therefore, both as parents and teachers, it is important to acquire items or games that reduce these unpleasant emotions. Items such as stress balls or a calm corner are usually very effective and easy to implement. We can find a place in the classroom or in their room that we will call "the calm corner" or a name that the child likes. In this space, we will place different items that the child may find pleasant. Remember that each child will find comfort in items that do not necessarily have to be shared with other children. You can put cushions, balls, and stress-relieving items, a Zen garden (with sand and a miniature rake for the child to comb the sand), etc. In short, you can put anything that helps the child calm down.

Exercise 7: The towel

The towel exercise is quite effective for self-regulation when we are very angry or furious about something that has happened to us. Anger arises when something seems unfair to us, when we have to do something we don't like, or when we have to stop doing something that motivates and entertains us. These three situations can provoke anger. To deal with anger, I sometimes suggest doing this exercise. It consists of placing a hand towel on the door handle or on the towel rack itself. We twist the towel while thinking about the event or person that has made us angry. When the towel can no longer be twisted any further, we let go and start again. Spending two to four minutes doing this exercise is usually very beneficial for the person. Let's be aware that whenever we experience the emotion of anger, we feel like attacking, and what better exercise than to do it with a towel and not direct our anger at someone else.

Exercise 8: Who's who of emotions

This is one of the most comprehensive exercises for working on emotion recognition. Do you remember the game *Guess Who* from your childhood? Well, this game consists of creating a similar game, but with emotions. Basic emotions (fear, anger, sadness, joy, disgust, surprise, etc.) are placed on a board or on individual cards, and the opponent's task is to guess the emotion. They will arrive at the answer by asking questions: Are their eyes wide open? Are they frowning?

Exercise 9: Draw your problem

Every time you feel a very intense emotion—such as fear, sadness, jealousy, anger, or boredom—try drawing what you feel on a piece of paper. Focus on the specific emotion you are feeling and draw it in great detail. You will see how much better you feel afterward.

Exercise 10: Improving my empathy

To finish the chapter on exercises to improve our self-regulation, think of a recent situation in which a friend or family member experienced something unpleasant. Reflect on it or answer the following questions:

a Describe in detail the situation your friend or family member was in:

____

____

b What emotion do you think that person was feeling (it could be several emotions)?

____

____

c What gestures and behaviors did they exhibit?

____

____

d Now focus on yourself. What emotions did you feel?

____

____

e What sensations did you notice?

____

____

f What thoughts did you have?

____

____

g What actions did you take?

____

____

h Having put yourself in the shoes of your family member or friend and then in your own, has your way of seeing and understanding what happened changed? Has your way of feeling about your family member or friend changed? What have you realized?

____

____

i Would you like to draw a picture of what happened? Go ahead.

Chapter 12

Exercises to develop processing speed

What is processing speed?

Processing speed is what we colloquially refer to as mental agility or quickness. Here, we can define it more technically as the number of units of information that our brain can handle at a given time. Now, we are going to focus on ten specific exercises to improve the processing speed of our children or students.

Exercise 1: The Usain Bolt of words

The following is a list of words. Your task is to read the following words as quickly as you can, but enunciating clearly.

Bird	Pencil	Towel
School	Car	Swing
Bicycle	Beach	Doll
Pen	fig	Book

DOI: 10.4324/9781003794332-12

Telephone	Watch	Dog
Chair	Window	Folder
Parrot	Park	Ball
Shirt	Cat	Computer
Child	Plate	Airplane
Lizard	Train	Stool

Exercise 2: In search of the lost symbol

Look closely at the first row of geometric shapes, where you will find a series of shapes with a symbol inside them. Your task is to draw the symbols that correspond to each geometric shape as you see them. Good luck!

Exercise 3: Speed reading

In Exercise 1, you had to read a series of words as quickly as possible. Now, you will have to read the following text as quickly as you can. Try to do it quickly, but pronounce all the words clearly and use intonation when necessary. Go ahead.

> When night fell, the owners of the little house returned. They were seven dwarfs who went out every day to work in the gold mines, far away in the heart of the mountains.
>
> "Wow, what a beautiful girl!" they exclaimed in surprise. "And how did she get here?"
>
> They approached her to admire her, taking care not to wake her. In the morning, Snow White was frightened when she woke up and saw the seven dwarfs surrounding her. They questioned her so gently that she calmed down and told them her sad story.
>
> Snow White and the Seven Dwarfs[1]

Exercise 4: Naming objects

Below, you will see a table with multiple objects and animals that you know well. Your task is to name them as quickly as possible. Time yourself to see how long it takes you to complete the entire exercise.

Exercise 5: Chess

For this exercise, we will need a chessboard and chess pieces. We will give the child all the chess pieces, and the task will be to place each piece in its place in the shortest time possible. If they are not familiar with chess, you can give them a photo or drawing of the placement of the pieces as a model. This game can be played with other games, such as Parcheesi and Goose. You can also give the child or teenager a whole deck of cards, and their task will be to sort them by suit (hearts, diamonds, spades, and clubs).

Exercise 6: The Little Coachman, Leré

The following is a list of words. Look at the model word: CAR. Your task is to read all the words as quickly as possible and circle those that contain the word CAR.

	Car	
CAR	CHOCO	CHOCHE
CAR	CAR	CAR
CAR	CAR	CECHO
CAR	CAR	CAR
OCHE	OCHE	COHCE
CHOCE	CAR	COHCE
CAR	CECHO	CAR
CAR	CAR	CECHO

Exercise 7: The horse

Next, you must count the total number of horses that appear in the following table as quickly as possible.

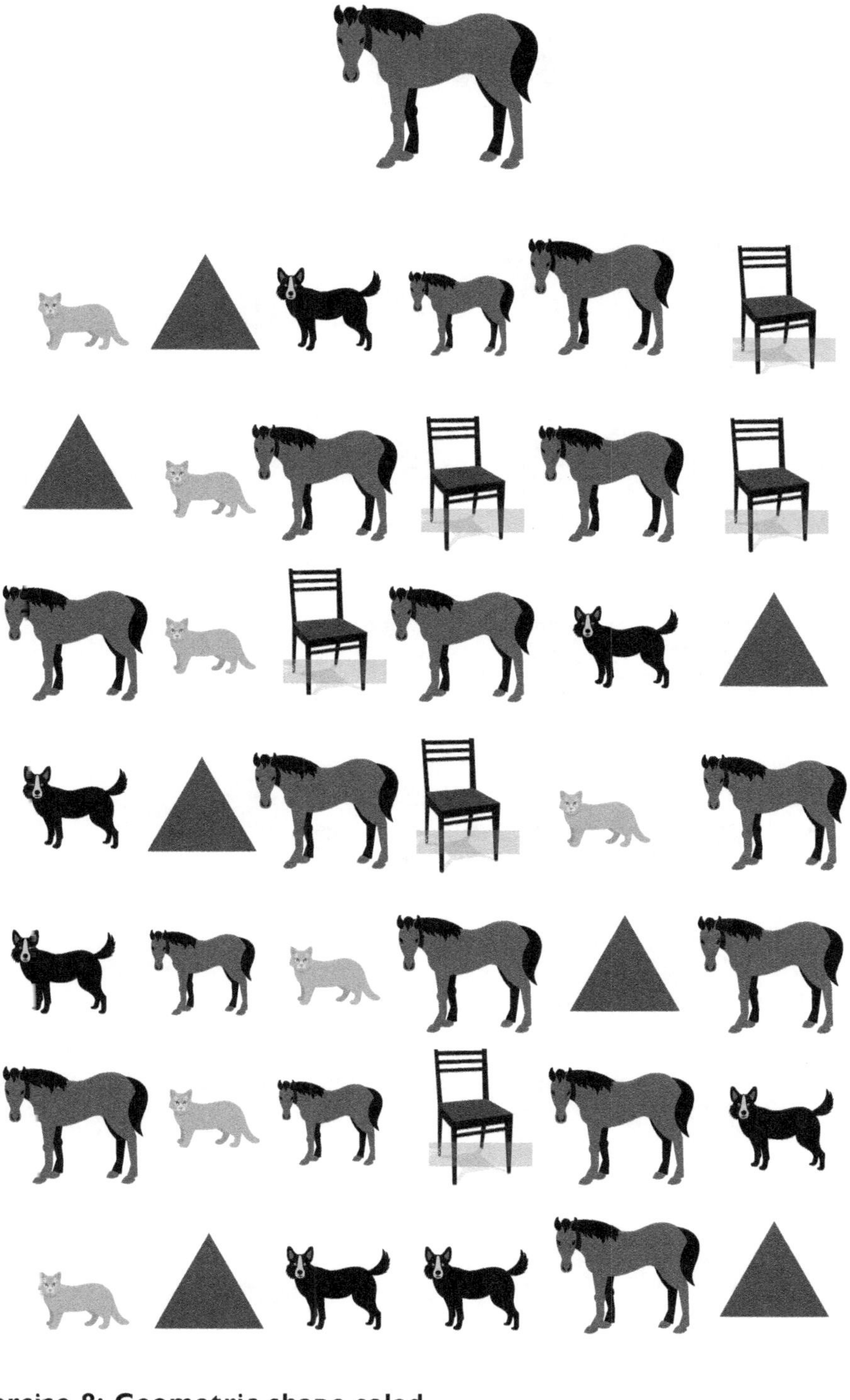

Exercise 8: Geometric shape salad

Try to name the geometric shapes below as quickly as possible.

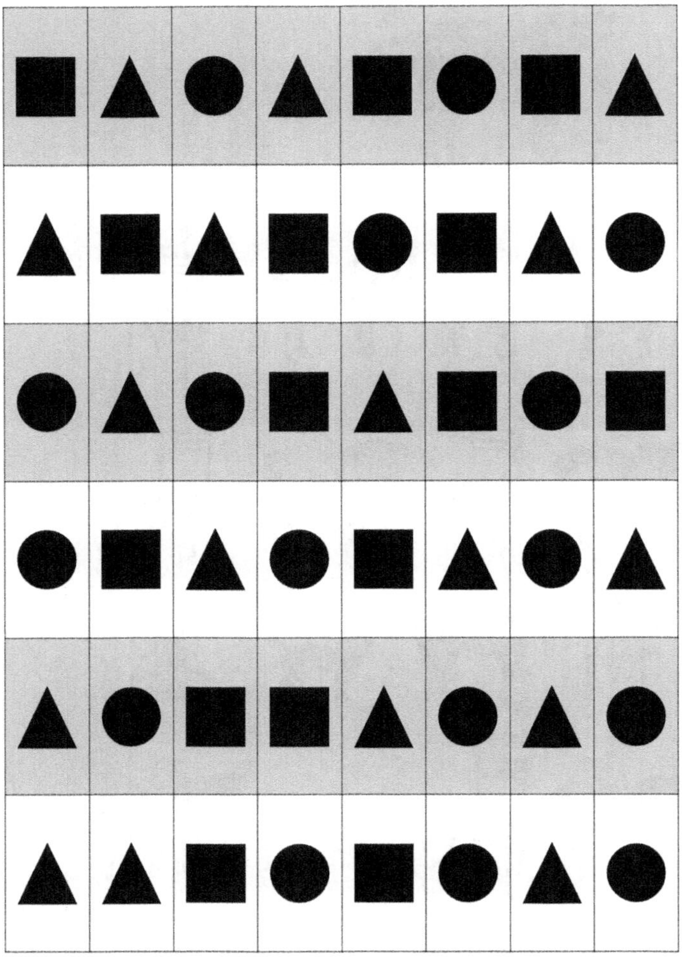

Exercise 9: The body in motion

To do this exercise, you will need to stand up. Read and carry out the following instructions as quickly as possible. An adult or partner can also read aloud the different tasks you must perform.

1 Two claps
2 Jump
3 One step to the right
4 Stomp
5 One clap
6 Stick out your tongue
7 Step back
8 Crouch
9 Jump
10 Crouch down
11 Three claps
12 Wave
13 Jump

14 Step to the left
15 Two claps
16 Crouch
17 Stick out your tongue
18 Touch your left ear
19 One clap
20 Jump

Exercise 10: Completing the child figure

Look at the model of the child we have drawn. Your task is to fill in the rest of the incomplete figures as quickly as possible. Remember to draw the child as he appears in the model. Go for it!

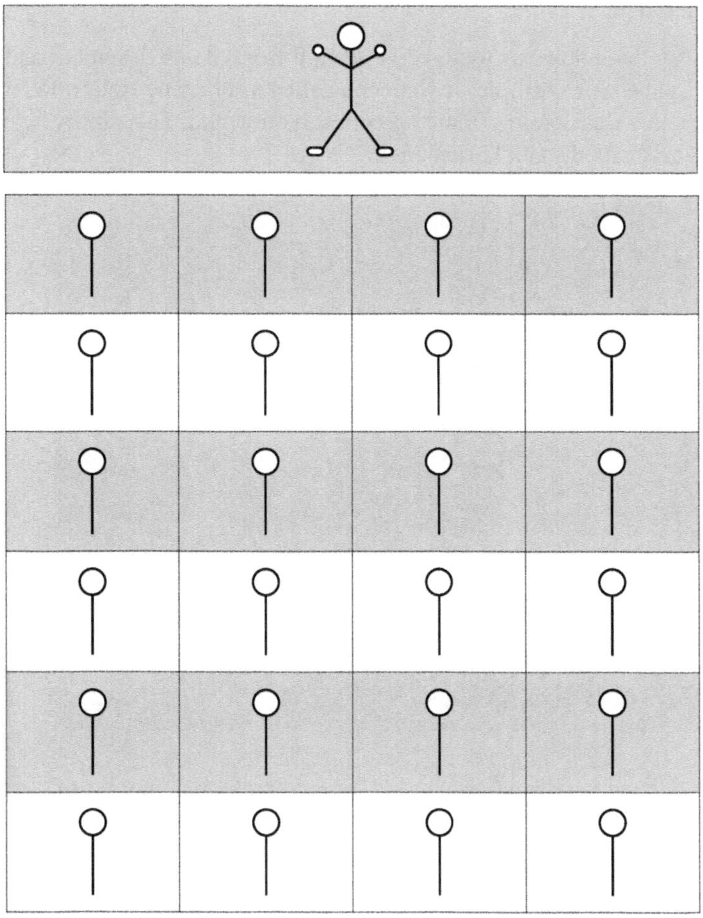

Note

1 Adapted from Jacob Grimm and Wilhelm Grimm, 'Little Snow-White,' in Household Tales, translated by Margaret Hunt. Public-domain text available via Project Gutenberg: https://us-east-2.protection.sophos.com?d=gutenberg.org&u=aHR0cHM6Ly93d3cuZ3V0ZW5iZXJnLm9yZy9lYm9va3MvNTMxNC7igJ0=&i=NjkyYzg3Yzg5MjMxZjQ2MDg4N2E3MzYz&t=L0JRNWpSS1FFa3pUVGNhOFJWNEpFazEyM2Q2RlhTci9MdEI5MGZTbnFrYz0=&h=10a50f1f483840109b8735acf37a72c0&s=AVNPUEhUT0NFTkNSWVBUSVbS5ncIZYzJLbOaQWUANYfRk4wJGjwRnK_tTVkQn0TcXg.

Chapter 13

Exercises to develop spatial orientation

What is spatial orientation?

Spatial orientation is the ability that allows us to perceive stimuli from the environment and process them to locate them in space. For example, if someone called your name right now, would you be able to tell where the voice was coming from? Of course, you would. This ability, which is trained from a very young age, is called spatial orientation.

Many activities and skills depend on spatial orientation. For example, reading, writing, counting, and mathematical calculation depend on the proper development of this skill. A difficulty or disorder in spatial orientation can cause problems with reading, handwriting, temporal sequences, mathematical calculation, etc.

Most common difficulties related to spatial orientation

Some of the difficulties our children and students may encounter are as follows:

- Difficulties in differentiating between left and right, up and down, inside and outside, etc.
- Poor integration of the body schema.

DOI: 10.4324/9781003794332-13

- They have difficulty identifying the part of the body that a person in front of them is moving.
- Sometimes, they do not copy drawings accurately.
- They often have difficulty with temporal sequences, puzzles, constructions, brain teasers, etc.
- They often confuse similar letters, for example, d-b, p-q, and m-n.
- Difficulties with organization, which often result in poor school planning.

Exercise 1: The triangles

Look closely at the model on the left. You have to place all the triangles you see in the model on the left into the table on the right in exactly the same position. Be careful and copy them exactly in the same place.

▲	▲		
		▲	
	▲		
		▲	

Along the same lines, but a little more complicated and for slightly older children, the following exercise can be used:

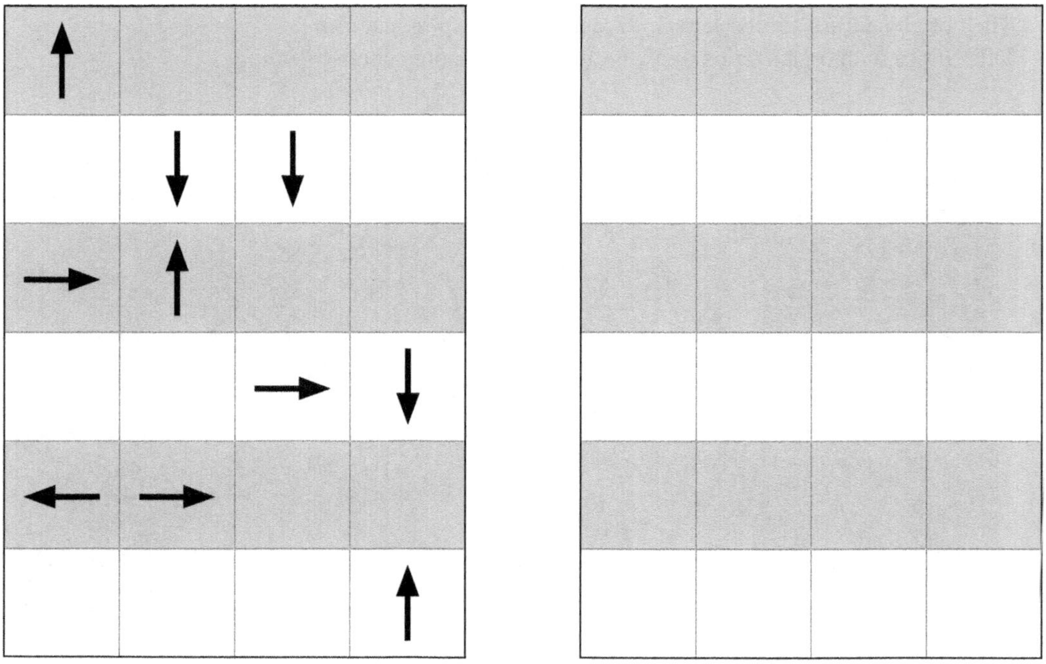

Exercise 2: Get your body moving!

Below are a series of short and simple instructions for your child or student. If you are a teacher, you can do this with the whole class at once (it's great fun). It is important that the person reading the instructions stands directly in front of the child, not behind or to the side. Let's do it.

1 Raise your right hand.
2 Raise your left hand.
3 Raise this hand (raise your left hand).
4 Raise this hand (raise your right hand).
5 Move your right ankle.
6 Move your left ankle.
7 Touch your left knee with your right hand.
8 Touch your right knee with your right hand.
9 Touch your right eye with your left thumb.
10 Point to my right eye.
11 Move your right ankle in a circular motion to the left.
12 Move your left ankle in a clockwise direction.
13 Raise your left hand with your eyes closed.
14 Touch your left knee with your left hand.

15 Touch your right knee with your left hand.
16 Touch your left eye with your right thumb.
17 Cover your mouth with your right hand.
18 Touch your right knee with your right hand.
19 Touch your left knee with your right hand.
20 Point to my left eye.
21 Raise your right hand with your eyes closed.
22 Move your right ankle in circles to the left.
23 Move your left ankle in a clockwise direction.
24 Cover your mouth with your left hand.
25 Wink at me with your right eye.

Exercise 3: Copy, copy!

Copy the figures below:

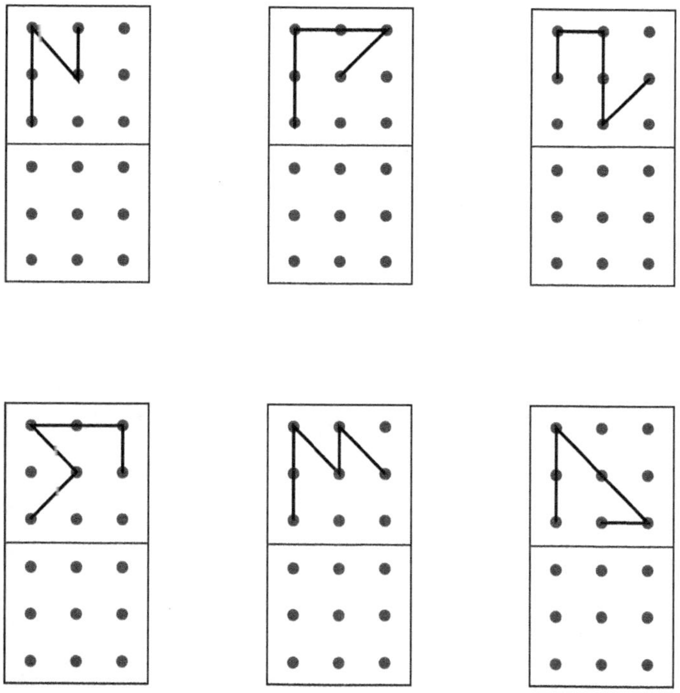

Exercise 4: The backpack and the ball

As you can see below, the backpack is associated with an upward arrow, while the ball is associated with a downward arrow. Your task is to draw the arrow in the correct direction under each backpack or ball. Go ahead!

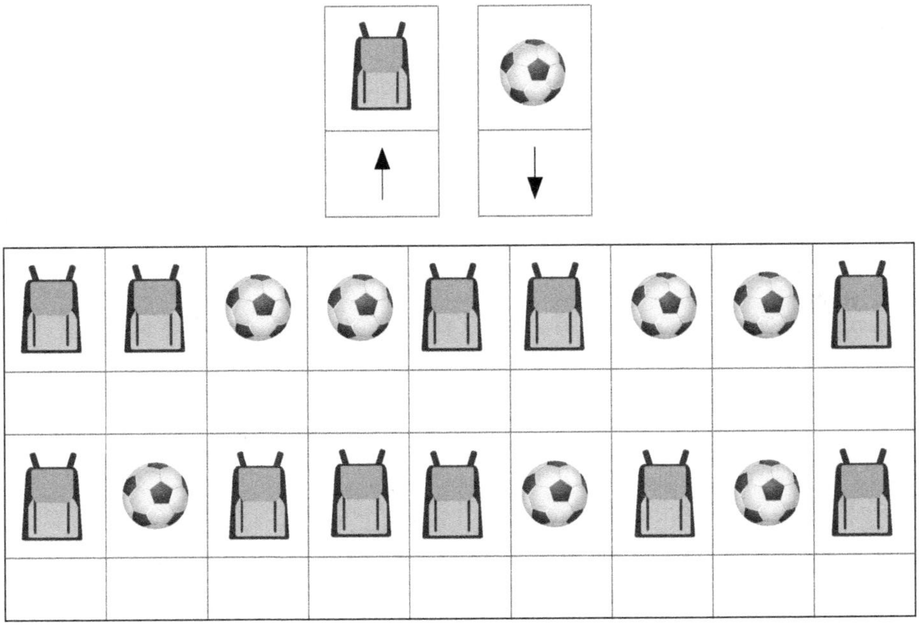

Exercise 5: Which way are they going?

Indicate which of the three drawings has the same orientation as the model. Circle the correct answer.

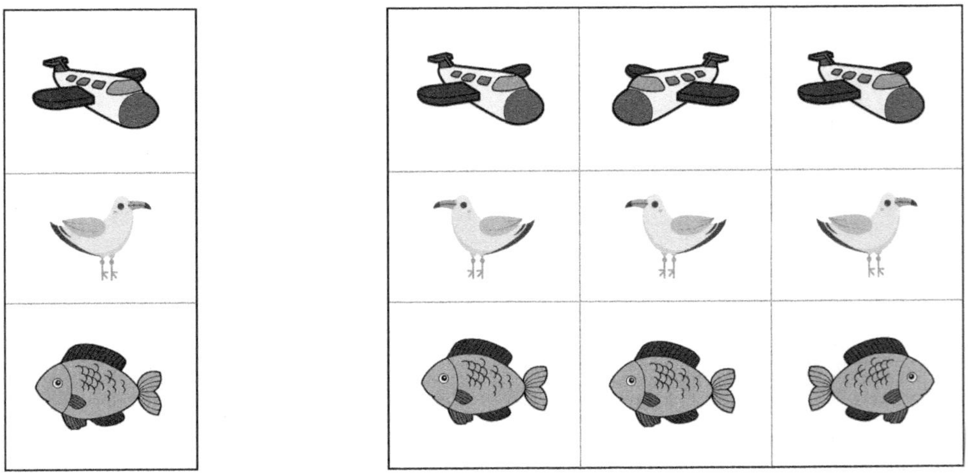

Exercise 6: The mystery letter

Look carefully at the following map. You must follow the instructions below to find out which mysterious letter we are looking for. Take into account the number of squares and the directions we give you to play the game correctly. Remember that the directions are given from your position.

1 Move two squares to the right.
2 Four squares down.
3 One square to the left.
4 Five squares up.
5 Four squares to the right.
6 One square up.
7 Three squares to the right.
8 One square down.
9 Two squares to the left.
10 Four squares down.

What is the mystery letter?

	B	A	D	N	F	F	H	K	A	L
	A	G	M	H	L	R	H	R	E	J
	D	T	G	A	M	T	E	Y	J	A
	D	M	T	A	G	L	J	S	Z	L
DEPARTURE →	V	S	T	S	H	E	U	G	A	H
	S	A	U	R	U	M	J	A	R	H
	R	J	R	U	D	Z	D	V	S	L
	O	V	O	A	V	H	A	T	E	D
	U	H	U	Z	Y	H	V	T	D	Ñ
	D	O	E	Y	T	H	E	H	H	M

Exercise 7: Curves

Have you seen the drawing we have shown you? First copy the drawing onto the grid, then copy it into the blank space.

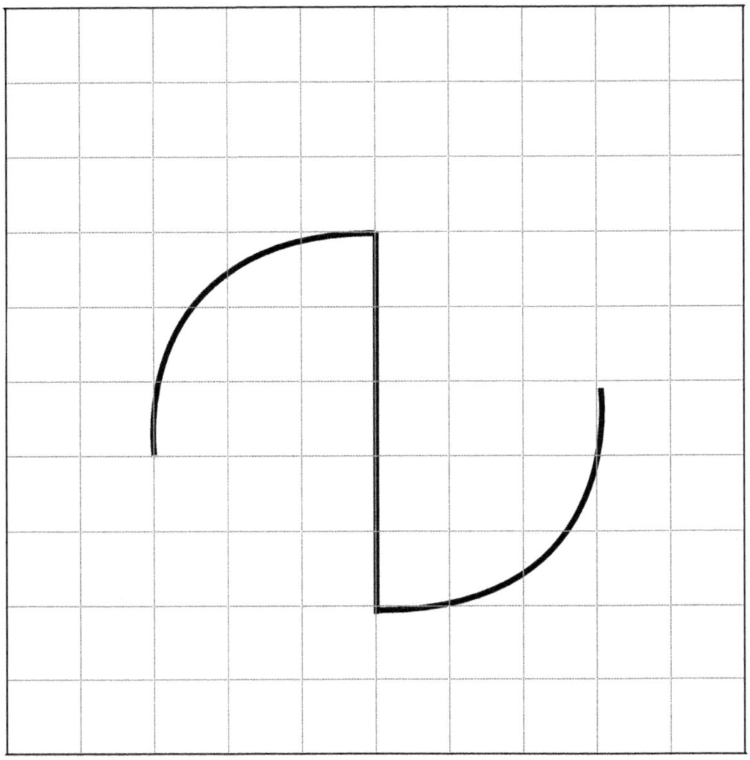

Exercise 8: The other half

Connect the dots to complete the missing half of the scissors.

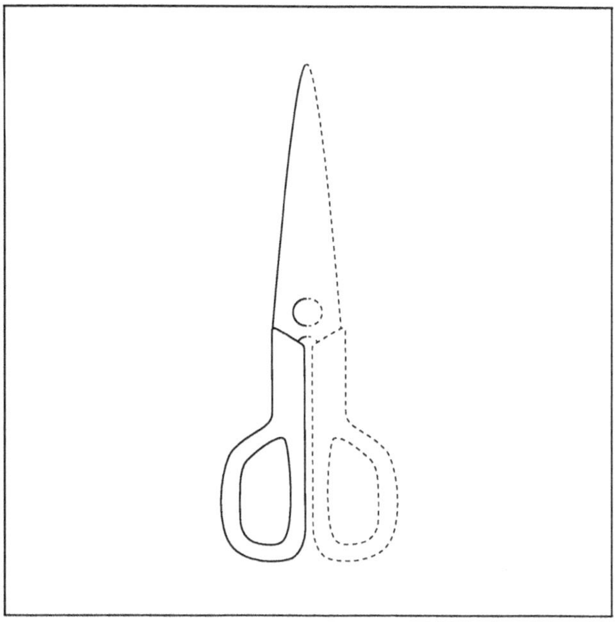

Now you must do the same as before, but this time you don't have as much help as in the previous exercise.

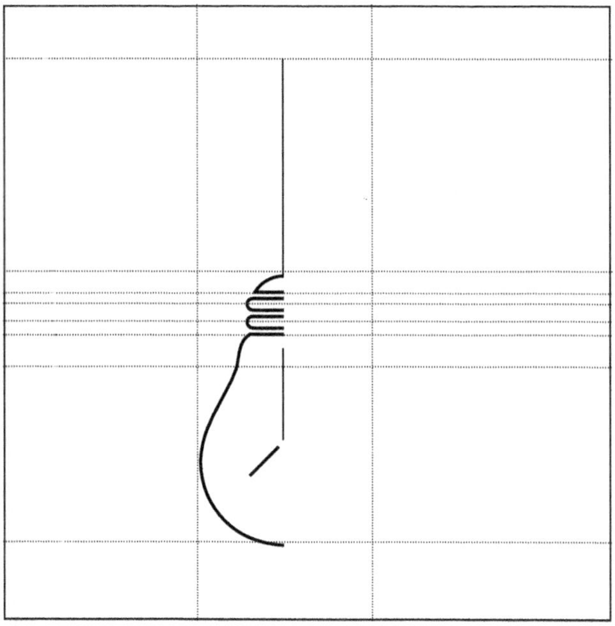

Exercise 9: Making cubes

Which of the four assembled cubes can be made from the net shown at the beginning?

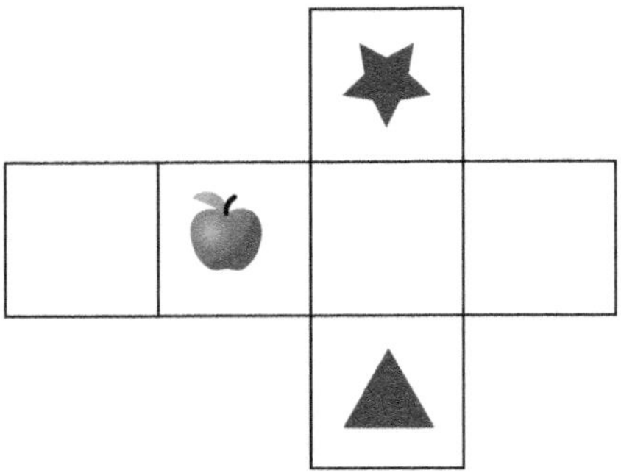

Exercise 10: Rubén, Clara, and Rosa

Look at the image below. There are three siblings: Rubén, Clara, and Rosa. You can also see some fruits. Answer the following questions:

1 What fruits are between Rubén and Clara?
2 Which fruit is farthest from Rosa?
3 What fruits are between Clara and Rosa?
4 Which fruit is farthest from Clara?
5 Which fruit is farthest away from Rubén?
6 Which brother is closest to the grapes?
7 Which brother is closest to the pineapple?

Chapter 14

Executive function disorders and difficulties

Lesions of the prefrontal cortex

For many years, medicine, psychology, and neuroscience did not study or treat the prefrontal cortex, as damage to it does not usually cause sensory or motor disorders. The vast majority of studies focused on language, learning, and memory. Today, the prefrontal cortex is one of the most studied areas of the brain. We have realized that this area plays an important role in the self-regulation of impulses, emotions, and thoughts. Currently, many of our children and students have difficulty controlling or inhibiting their impulses. Training in executive functions improves this performance.

Although damage to the prefrontal cortex does not usually cause sensory or motor difficulties, other psychological functions are often impaired, such as organization, sustained attention, and mathematical calculation. All of these processes are voluntary and conscious.

The anterior part of the brain is at greater risk of traumatic damage simply because of its location. Accidents, blows, and trauma are some examples. For this reason, cases of children with alterations in the prefrontal cortex, known as *dysexecutive syndrome*, are relatively common, which we will discuss in the following section. In dysexecutive syndrome, one or more executive functions may be impaired, placing the child in a situation of significant dependence. Imagine for a moment what it would be like, for example, to be unable to concentrate on a book or movie for more than a minute, or your memory not retaining the information you are given in a work meeting. It would be utter chaos that would make us very dependent. This is how children and adults with prefrontal cortex difficulties feel. But the prefrontal cortex can also be altered by infectious, pharmacological, toxic, or tumorous processes, among others.

DOI: 10.4324/9781003794332-14

Executive dysfunction, or executive function disorders, can be caused by three general factors:

- **Structural**: The structure of the brain or a specific part of the brain is different when compared to a neurotypical brain.
- **Functional**: The brain functions differently from what is considered normal.
- **Connectivity (neurotransmitters)**: The connection between different neural groups is different due to an excess or deficit of certain neurotransmitters.

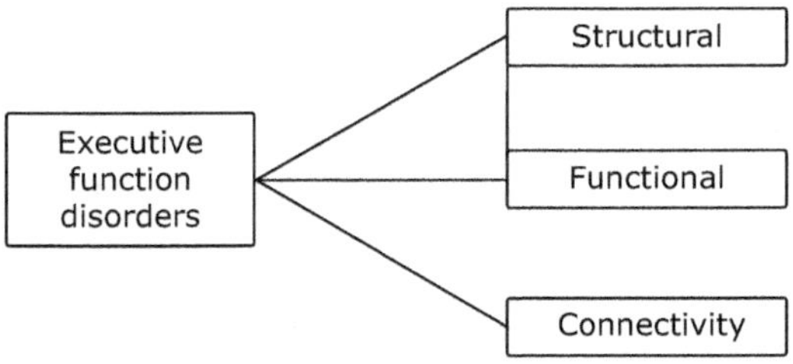

Dysexecutive syndrome

Dysexecutive syndrome is defined as a set of cognitive, emotional, and behavioral disorders in children caused by an explicit lesion or dysfunction of the prefrontal lobes or their connections with the rest of the brain. Some of the characteristics of children or adults with dysexecutive syndrome are as follows:

- Difficulty achieving goals.
- Slowing of processing speed.
- Difficulty regulating emotions.
- Inability to categorize or abstract ideas from a text or story.
- Difficulty planning, anticipating, monitoring, or inhibiting mental activity.
- Loss of ability to concentrate.
- Lack of cognitive flexibility; they maintain very rigid attitudes.
- Changes in personality, mood, and emotional control. They behave like children or as impulsive and uninhibited people.
- Difficulties in reasoning and decision-making.
- They tend to lack internal language.
- They sometimes display aggressive, impulsive behavior and experience constant mood swings, even when there is no apparent reason.

Therefore, the vast majority of impaired functions in dysexecutive syndrome are the executive functions that we have been looking at throughout the book.

The vast majority of research conducted on dysexecutive syndrome has been carried out on children diagnosed with attention deficit hyperactivity disorder (ADHD), as demonstrated by studies by Barkley, Biederman, and Faraone, among others. Research by psychologist Francisco Xavier Castellanos concludes that children and adolescents with ADHD have a dysfunction in the fronto-striatal-cerebellar circuit, that is, in the highway that connects the prefrontal cortex with the emotional brain and the reptilian brain. This is why children with ADHD are so impulsive and have such difficulty controlling and managing their emotions. We will discuss all of this in more detail in the section on ADHD.

An injury or accident in the prefrontal cortex results in the manifestation of a series of symptoms. This set of symptoms is generically referred to as *dysexecutive syndrome*. This syndrome usually occurs when injuries occur in the cerebral cortex (rational brain) rather than in the subcortex (emotional or reptilian brain). Accidents or injuries to the prefrontal cortex normally cause difficulties in executive functioning and attention control, as well as affect other executive processes.

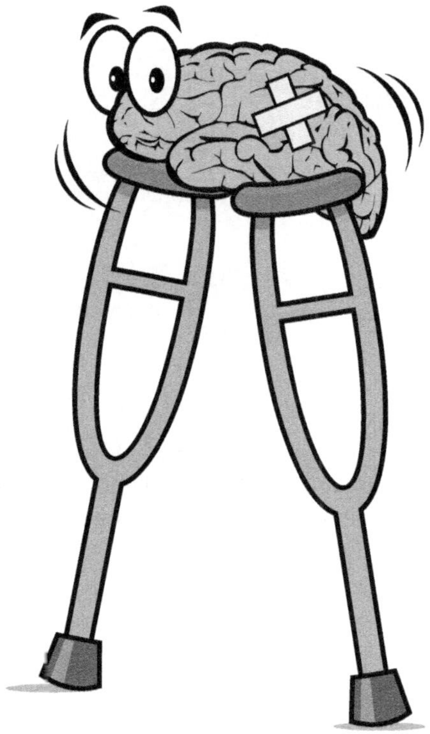

There are several psychiatric disorders that involve difficulties in some of the executive functions we have discussed. Some examples are as follows:

- Obsessive-compulsive disorder (OCD)
- Behavioral disorders
- Epilepsy
- Addictions
- Schizophrenia
- Traumatic brain injury
- ADHD
- Alzheimer's disease
- Huntington's disease

All of these disorders have common symptoms, such as impulsivity, lack of perseverance, difficulty concentrating, cognitive rigidity, and difficulties in self-regulating emotions and behavior.

As has been observed, many dysexecutive syndromes are associated with pathologies or disorders in children and, therefore, are encountered in the school environment. How does this executive difficulty affect children in the academic setting? These children often have difficulties with reading comprehension and writing, problems with mathematics, difficulties in studying and acquiring new concepts, problems when doing assignments and exams, etc.

The curious case of Phineas Gage

The first documented case of what we now know as executive dysfunction syndrome is that of Phineas Gage. Gage, a Welsh miner, was injured in a workplace accident while building a railroad in Vermont, USA, in 1848. A metal rod pierced his entire orbitofrontal area. In the following lateral image of the brain, we can see the area that was pierced by the rod.

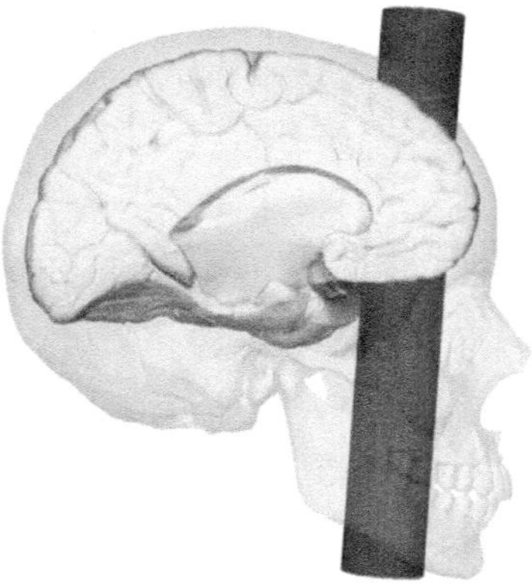

As we mentioned earlier, injuries to the prefrontal cortex do not usually affect basic sensory and motor functions, but they do affect executive functions. After the accident, Phineas Gage went from being a good, responsible, and caring worker to being rude, impulsive, capricious, and unable to manage his impulses and emotions. He went from having a brain that functioned holistically to having a brain only capable of accelerating (lower and hot brains) but not of braking (prefrontal cortex). Thirteen years after his accident, he died.

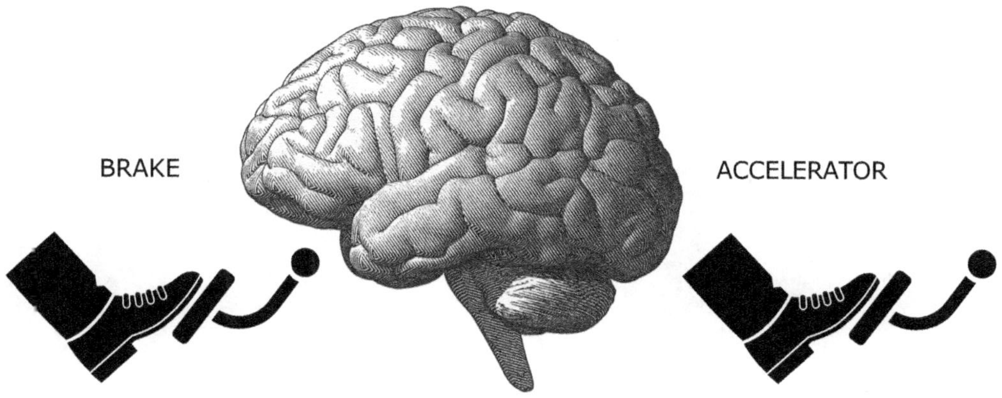

Depending on which area of the prefrontal cortex is affected, a series of symptoms or manifestations may occur. Lesions in the dorsolateral and medial areas will have a greater impact on the child's cognitive processes, while lesions in the orbitofrontal area will have more emotional and motivational consequences. In dysexecutive syndrome and in prefrontal cortex lesions in general, concentration is usually impaired, especially sustained attention and alternating attention. It is normal for these children, when doing a task or activity, to pay attention to other stimuli that are not relevant at that precise moment, as their impulse control is also affected.

Attention deficit hyperactivity disorder, better known by its acronym ADHD, is one of the disorders that most affects children. ADHD is a neurodevelopmental disorder, which means that the brains of affected children mature more slowly than those of other children of the same age. This immaturity is most visible in certain areas of the brain, particularly the prefrontal cortex, which is responsible for executive functions such as impulse control, planning, and concentration, among others. The two brain neurotransmitters that are altered in people with ADHD are dopamine and norepinephrine.

The main difficulty with ADHD lies in executive functions. As explained in the chapter on concentration, it is not that children with ADHD lack focus, but rather that their focus is constantly shifting, making it very difficult for them to concentrate on a task for a long period of time.

The main symptoms or manifestations of this disorder can vary greatly depending on the child, their age, and the subtype of ADHD present. The core symptoms of this disorder are attention deficit, hyperactivity, and impulsivity, but this does not mean that all children with this condition have all three main symptoms. In addition, there are a number of secondary symptoms of ADHD, which are as follows:

- Difficulties in regulating emotions
- Poor working memory
- Difficulties in internal time control
- Poor task planning skills
- Difficulties with internal language

- Low tolerance for frustration
- Cognitive rigidity
- Constant need for external reinforcement

All of these symptoms will manifest themselves to a greater or lesser extent in the different environments or contexts in which the child or adolescent develops. Let's look at the environments in which the symptoms usually manifest themselves, as well as some relevant information about each of them:

- **Academic setting**: Parents of children with ADHD have a higher number of parent-teacher conferences at school than parents of other children in the class. In addition, children with ADHD are four to five times more likely to receive specific treatments both inside and outside of school.
- **Family environment**: Parents of children with ADHD tend to have more doubts about their ability to parent and are up to four times more likely to separate than other families.
- **Social sphere**: Between 60% and 70% of children diagnosed with ADHD are rejected and stigmatized by their peers because of their symptoms. Seventy percent of them admit to not having any best friends and are often less likely to be invited to birthday parties.
- **Emotional sphere**: They tend to have great difficulty identifying and understanding their own emotions and those of others. In addition, a very high percentage of children with ADHD have low self-esteem.
- **Behavioral**: Children and adolescents with ADHD exhibit a greater number of risky behaviors and, therefore, are more likely to have accidents and die than other children their age.

- **Executive function**: They perform worse on tests of concentration, planning, impulse control (inhibition), and working memory. We have already mentioned that ADHD is a problem that directly affects the prefrontal cortex and, therefore, executive functions.

The vast majority of studies conclude that the prevalence of ADHD, that is, the percentage of the child population diagnosed with this disorder, is around 5–7%. The etiology (cause) of this disorder is mainly genetic. Stephen Faraone's studies conclude that genetic factor accounts for 77% of ADHD's etiology. Thus, it is the disorder with the greatest DNA influence that exists, exceeding depression (39%) and generalized anxiety (32%).

There are three different manifestations or subtypes of ADHD: inattentive, hyperactive-impulsive, and combined (inattentive and hyperactive-impulsive). At what age is ADHD usually detected or diagnosed? Generally, the inattentive subtype takes the longest to detect because its symptoms are less visible (attention deficit). It is usually detected around ages 8–9, if not later. The hyperactive-impulsive and combined subtypes are usually detected earlier (around ages 5–7) because their symptoms are more observable. Even so, studies by Willcutt (2012) conclude that the most common subtype of ADHD is the inattentive subtype, even though the most commonly diagnosed subtype is the combined subtype.

Emotions in daily life

Executive functions are not affected only in people with executive dysfunction syndrome; those of us who do not have this syndrome may also find ourselves in situations where executive functioning is poor or even absent.

Whenever we experience intense emotions, such as anger, sadness, or even joy, our emotional brain takes control and overrides the prefrontal cortex. It is as if the coachman of the carriage (prefrontal cortex) falls asleep (inhibition of the prefrontal cortex) and leaves the reins to the horses (emotions). The horses then go wherever they want, while reason is inhibited.

Think about our behavior when we are in love. What about when we are very angry with someone? What about when we are under the influence of alcohol? In all these everyday examples, we act similarly to a child or to a person with dysexecutive syndrome. Emotions (the horses) take control of our behavior. The limbic system is activated, and the prefrontal cortex is inhibited or numbed.

As we age, some of our mental abilities are affected. The processing speeds and rhythms also slow down. Think of the neurological impairments associated with old age. Older people have greater difficulty concentrating, controlling their impulses, memorizing, learning, etc.

Reference

Willcutt, E. G. (2012). The prevalence of DSM-IV attention-deficit/hyperactivity disorder: A meta-analytic review. *Neurotherapeutics*, 9(3), 490–499. https://doi.org/10.1007/s13311-012-0135-8

Chapter 15

Design of executive function training

Historical background of intervention programs

Training or stimulation in executive functions aims to maximize the executive resources of the child or adult being worked with by exercising the most deficient functions.

The first cognitive rehabilitation training programs appeared shortly after the end of World War I. The goal was to improve the quality of life of soldiers who had suffered various types of brain injuries during the war. Alexander Luria was the driving force behind cognitive rehabilitation beginning in the 1960s.

In the following section, we will look at the characteristics that an executive training or cognitive stimulation program must have in order to be effective and achieve the expected results in children or students. The ideas presented below are the basis for a proper program or training in executive functions with children who do not have a significant impairment in their executive functioning. To do this, we can look at all the exercises that have been proposed so far for each of the executive functions. In the event of a significant difficulty or delay, this task should not be carried out by a family member or teacher. In such situations, it is always advisable to consult a professional (neuropsychologist, psychologist, etc.) to assess the child in question and implement an individualized program.

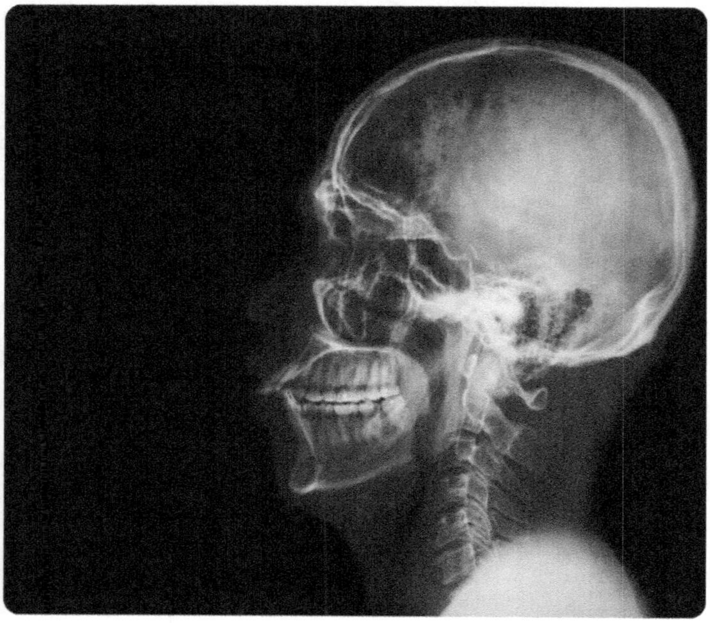

DOI: 10.4324/9781003794332-15

Basic principles of training in executive functions

When designing or preparing a cognitive stimulation program, we must take into account a series of basic principles on which the program should be based. Let's take a look at these principles:

- **Age of the person we are working with.** The younger the person we are working with, the greater the results of the intervention in executive functions will be. This fact is based on the principle of brain plasticity, which we explained in the first chapter.
- **Program customization.** We must adapt cognitive training to the personal characteristics of the child or group with whom we are going to work. We cannot use standard programs based solely on the child's diagnosis. For example, there is no standard or single program for working with children diagnosed with ADHD or dyslexia.

- **Conduct the different training sessions on a regular basis.** It is better to train a little every day than to train one day a week for several hours.
- **Exercises should be brief.** Exercises should not last too long because it could tire the child. Short sessions help optimize concentration during cognitive training and allow us to make much better use of the time.
- **Dynamic and engaging activities.** Executive training that is monotonous, demotivating, and in which the child has a passive role ends up being ineffective. Sometimes training in executive functions is designed in a rigid way without taking into account the idiosyncratic characteristics

of the child or group, which makes executive stimulation ineffective. The important thing is not the method used, but the child with whom we are working.

- **Immediate feedback.** Whenever we do an activity or exercise with a child, it is very important that we let them know how they did. This will increase the child's motivation. We should point out both the mistakes the child makes and the successes the child has throughout the training session.

- **Variability.** It is important that the different training sessions we design to work on executive functions with the child are as varied as possible. We can use paper-and-pencil exercises, other activities, such as counting and intelligence games, computer games, and auditory, tactile, and visual games.
- **Use different sensory channels.** If we use different sensory channels in executive training, we facilitate the practice of executive functions. We can give children exercises and activities using visual, auditory, visual-auditory, kinesthetic, and tactile presentation. An example of visual-auditory stimulation is having the child read a series of letters that appear in a word search in an orderly manner. Each time they see a vowel, they tap on the table. We know that using several sensory channels simultaneously increases and reinforces learning.
- **In cases of brain damage, we must bear in mind that spontaneous recovery of the executive functions we want to improve occurs more actively during the weeks following the accident.** If we are working with a child who has suffered an injury affecting executive functions due to trauma, we must be aware that this phenomenon tends to diminish over time. Therefore, improvement in executive functions will occur in the period immediately following the brain damage or accident.

Practical characteristics of executive function training

We will now outline the characteristics needed to make our proposed intervention in executive functions effective for a child or a group of children. These characteristics are based on the basic principles discussed in the previous section. We have summarized the characteristics of an executive training program in the following ten points:

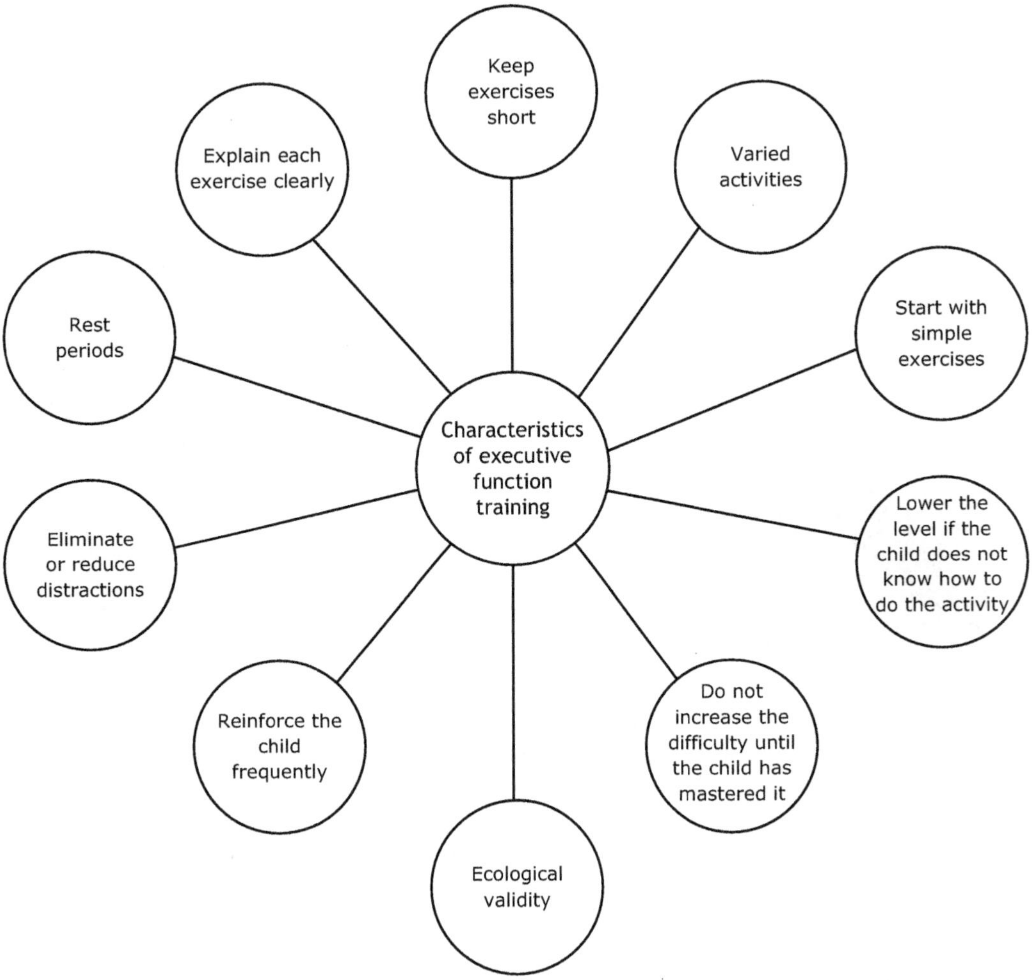

1 **Short training sessions and exercises.** Ideally, they should last between 15 and 30 minutes and be conducted early in the morning. Try to conduct the training when the brain is fresh.
2 **The activities should be varied.** If we always work on concentration through crossing-out exercises or planning through mazes, the child may eventually become bored. We must, therefore, use different exercises to keep the child motivated.
3 **Always start training sessions with simple exercises.** The aim of starting with simple exercises is to encourage the child's adherence and self-efficacy.

4 **Lower the level of difficulty if the child is unable to perform a certain exercise.**

5 **Do not increase the difficulty level of the exercise until the child has mastered the previous level.** It is important to proceed step by step, from easier to more difficult tasks. Therefore, it is beneficial to leave the most complex tasks for the end of the training session.

6 **Ecological validity.** The closer the activity is to the child's reality, the better. For example, if we want to work on the working memory of a group of children, what better way to train it than to set up a market where they go shopping at different stalls.

7 **Reinforce the child's efforts and inform the child of the results they are achieving.** It is very important to give them *feedback* on how they are doing.

8 **Reduce or eliminate any potential distractions in the room or classroom.** Sometimes this is impossible, but we should try to reduce them as much as possible so that concentration is maximized and the work is as effective as possible.

9 **Establish rest periods.** If necessary, take breaks so that the child can rest between activities. Allowing the brain to rest is always beneficial.

10 **Simplicity.** Explain each exercise in the simplest way possible so that the child understands it. Once you have explained what to do, it is important to check that the child understands and to let them ask any questions they may have before starting the training session.

Web resources for working on executive functions

In this section, you will find links to some websites that may be of interest when working on certain executive functions with your children or students. I did not want to make the list too exhaustive, so this is a selection of the most interesting resources. In the additional content of the book, which can be downloaded with the code on the first page, you will find these links for easier access.

Impulse control

https://www.wordgames.com/game/4-pix-word-quiz
https://www.cognifit.com/aplicaciones/html5/brain/game/whack-a-mole/l/en
https://www.cognifit.com/aplicaciones/html5/brain/game/bee-balloon/l/en

Planning

https://www.ravensburger.us/en-US/products/games/thinkfun/rush-hour-76582
https://www.sesamestreet.org/games

Puzzles

https://www.jigsawplanet.com/

Cognitive flexibility

https://www.cognifit.com/brain-games/bee-balloon

Websites with various games

http://www.gamesforthebrain.com/;

Chapter 16

The ten best board games for working on executive functions

Many board games are effective for developing different executive functions. Practically any board game, from traditional favorites to more innovative titles, can help strengthen children's concentration, planning, working memory, and emotional self-regulation. The aim of this chapter is to introduce a selection of games beyond the classics we all know. Chess, dominoes, cinquillo (a traditional Spanish card game), the Game of the Goose, and Parcheesi are familiar games that we played with our parents and now play with our children, and they are extremely effective. Here, I focus on other games that may be less familiar because they are more recent additions to the market. I hope you enjoy them and find these suggestions useful.

Exercise 1: Fast Flags®

This is one of my favorite exercises for working on concentration, planning, and, above all, processing speed. It's also a fun way to learn about some of the flags of the world. All the cards are dealt among the participants, and the winner is the one who runs out of cards first. To discard cards, at least two flags on the same side must match the flags on the card on the table. I'm sure you'll enjoy it.

Exercise 2: The little clock

This is a very simple and effective game for working on impulse control. The more players, the more fun you'll have. I usually play with a Spanish deck of cards. All the cards are dealt out to the players. With the cards face down, each player takes turns throwing down a card while singing the hours of the clock: one, two, three, four…

If the card you play matches the number we are going for, you win all the cards. But be careful, you must pay attention to both your cards and those of your teammates because if you make a mistake and the next player doesn't notice, they will win the cards.

Exercise 3: Speed Cups®

Speed Cups® is a game designed primarily to improve cognitive flexibility. It is a very simple game. It consists of small cubes in five different colors (blue, red, yellow, green, and black) that must be arranged either vertically or horizontally, depending on the card you are dealt. Hurry up and arrange the cubes correctly!

DOI: 10.4324/9781003794332-16

Exercise 4: Cruel World®

One of the best ways to work on theory of mind and empathy is with Mundo Cruel® (Cruel World). This is a series of cards with very unusual and cruel scenes. On the back of each card, there is a series of questions to ask the participants. To avoid automatic responses from children or adolescents, unusual images are used to force participants to think.

Exercise 5: Dobble®

Perhaps you are familiar with this game. It has been very popular in recent years, and children (and adults) love it. The round cards in the game are eye-catching, as they are filled with objects. The task is to find the object that is repeated on the two cards placed on the table. Be careful, because there is always a repeated object or stimulus, even if it is not immediately obvious and you have a hard time finding it.

Exercise 6: Emotion!®

It is a card game created by the El Perruco group, and it is very useful for developing a broad emotional vocabulary. There are a total of 60 cards, each representing an emotion. In total, there are 12 families of emotions. Each family has five cards with different intensities of the emotion, ranging from the mildest (1) to the most intense (5). It can be played in many ways, but the important thing is that it gives the player the opportunity to learn about a wide range of emotions.

Exercise 7: Cortex Challenge®

It is one of the most comprehensive board games I have seen in recent years. There are eight different tests in total: memory, mazes, color, coordination, repetition, frequency, reasoning, and tactile challenge. Thanks to these eight tests, we can stimulate and work on different executive functions in a fun way.

A very comprehensive game!

Exercise 8: Touch and Find®

This game is used to work on the participants' *gnosis* (perception). It can be used with young children from 2½ to 3 years of age. Players have to put their hands into a covered bucket and recognize the different objects they are touching by their shape. All the objects are familiar and everyday items, but recognizing them by touch without being able to see them makes the task quite difficult. Some of the objects that participants must recognize are a cloud, car, motorcycle, moon, crocodile, and eggplant.

Exercise 9: Ghost Blitz®

The ghost Balduin found an old camera that could make objects disappear when he photographed them. Unfortunately, the camera was haunted, and the colors of the objects he photographed were not always true to life. In each round, a card is turned over. Players must identify and grab the correct object as quickly as possible. The player who responds correctly wins the card, and the player with the most cards at the end wins. It is an engaging game for working on impulse control.

Exercise 10: Mikado®

Just as we previously recommended a game to develop children's and students' gnosis (perception), we now recommend Mikado® to work on praxias. Among other skills, it develops fine motor control, concentration, and impulse control. The game begins when one player gathers all the sticks and drops them onto the table. Players then take turns removing the sticks one by one without moving any of the others. If a player moves another stick while attempting to remove one, their turn ends. The differently colored sticks have different point values, and the player with the most points wins.

Solutions

(i) Chapter 5: Exercises to develop concentration

(a) Exercise 1: The imperial eagle

- Ages: 4–5
- Solution:

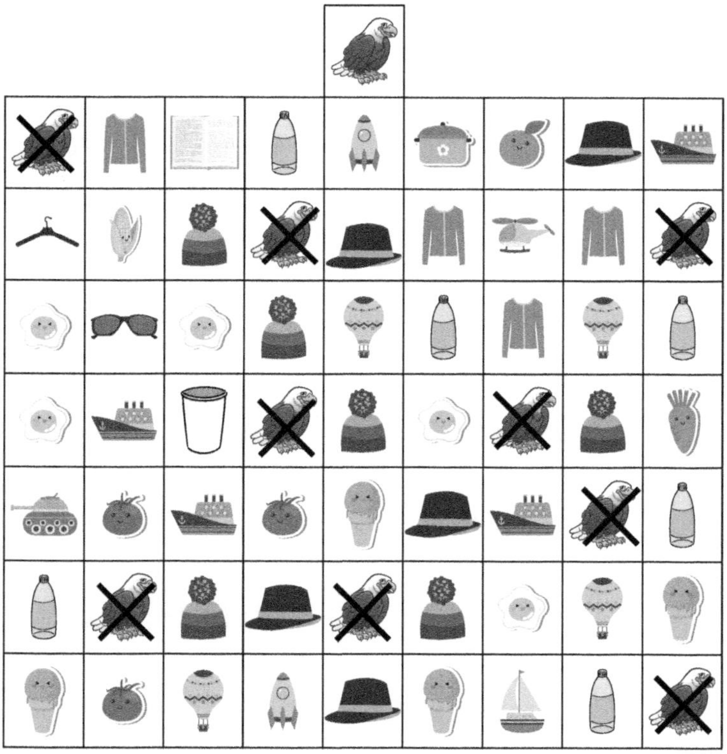

(b) *Exercise 2: In search of the lost vowels*

- Ages: 5–6 years old
- Solution:

J	g	i	m	L	u	y	B	e	Q	y	l
B	a	f	b	n	a	i	N	B	T	U	u
G	Q	q	f	j	J	A	b	A	y	d	c
r	j	u	L	E	T	a	h	G	l	G	f
a	t	H	M	e	l	i	d	I	J	t	N
h	I	J	B	U	F	L	J	i	Q	r	e
b	i	q	a	R	j	d	A	f	e	U	q
Q	a	t	i	H	t	e	n	u	j	y	n
A	m	R	u	d	B	m	r	T	F	i	u
f	e	d	B	N	q	d	q	i	d	j	l
h	M	l	a	u	h	M	I	j	a	A	n
B	Y	F	H	L	J	N	t	R	l	F	L
u	Q	y	b	D	M	E	e	a	m	q	D

(c) *Exercise 3: The letter game*

- Ages: 7
- Solution:

N	X	E	A	P	W	H	V	A	Q	H	R	Y	A	K	O	G	M	A	Z	L	Q
A	F	Z	R	U	A	I	I	I	S	C	X	I	P	W	B	A	Q	B	D	G	A
Q	I	0	G	A	V	K	Y	D	U	A	A	B	Z	T	P	J	A	L	R	M	C
B	A	L	P	K	R	A	J	E	I	0	Z	H	V	X	A	Q	F	W	S	A	U
T	I	S	A	F	M	Z	V	A	K	L	B	U	A	R	I	H	P	A	0	B	X
F	N	R	E	W	C	A	H	T	Y	Q	M	J	S	D	I	Z	V	K	I	G	L
U	A	I	Z	X	A	0	B	I	I	T	G	P	Y	C	W	A	E	R	H	A	N
L	V	A	J	P	S	R	K	I	A	B	N	A	F	X	U	M	Q	D	A	C	W
0	K	Q	D	C	M	H	W	G	B	V	R	S	B	I	L	Z	T	Y	F	U	J
Y	Z	A	U	T	I	G	T	S	A	J	0	A	D	P	H	N	R	M	A	E	V
E	A	W	H	R	A	L	T	B	M	D	V	I	G	0	S	A	K	U	X	A	P
R	T	P	Y	N	K	A	S	W	L	U	C	Q	E	H	A	F	B	J	0	Z	I
H	B	K	A	G	0	C	E	A	P	R	I	W	A	U	Q	L	D	A	T	S	Y
D	A	J	S	I	L	A	N	F	R	E	P	C	H	V	A	0	G	T	B	A	K
C	Q	T	B	A	E	W	O	R	J	A	A	L	I	M	D	S	A	H	G	K	F
A	L	G	I	D	A	S	M	B	I	H	R	U	E	J	A	0	F	P	C	N	A
S	E	H	A	B	W	I	P	A	G	Z	I	K	A	Q	Y	R	C	A	U	I	M

(d) Exercise 4: Clap your hands

- Ages: 6–7
- Solution:

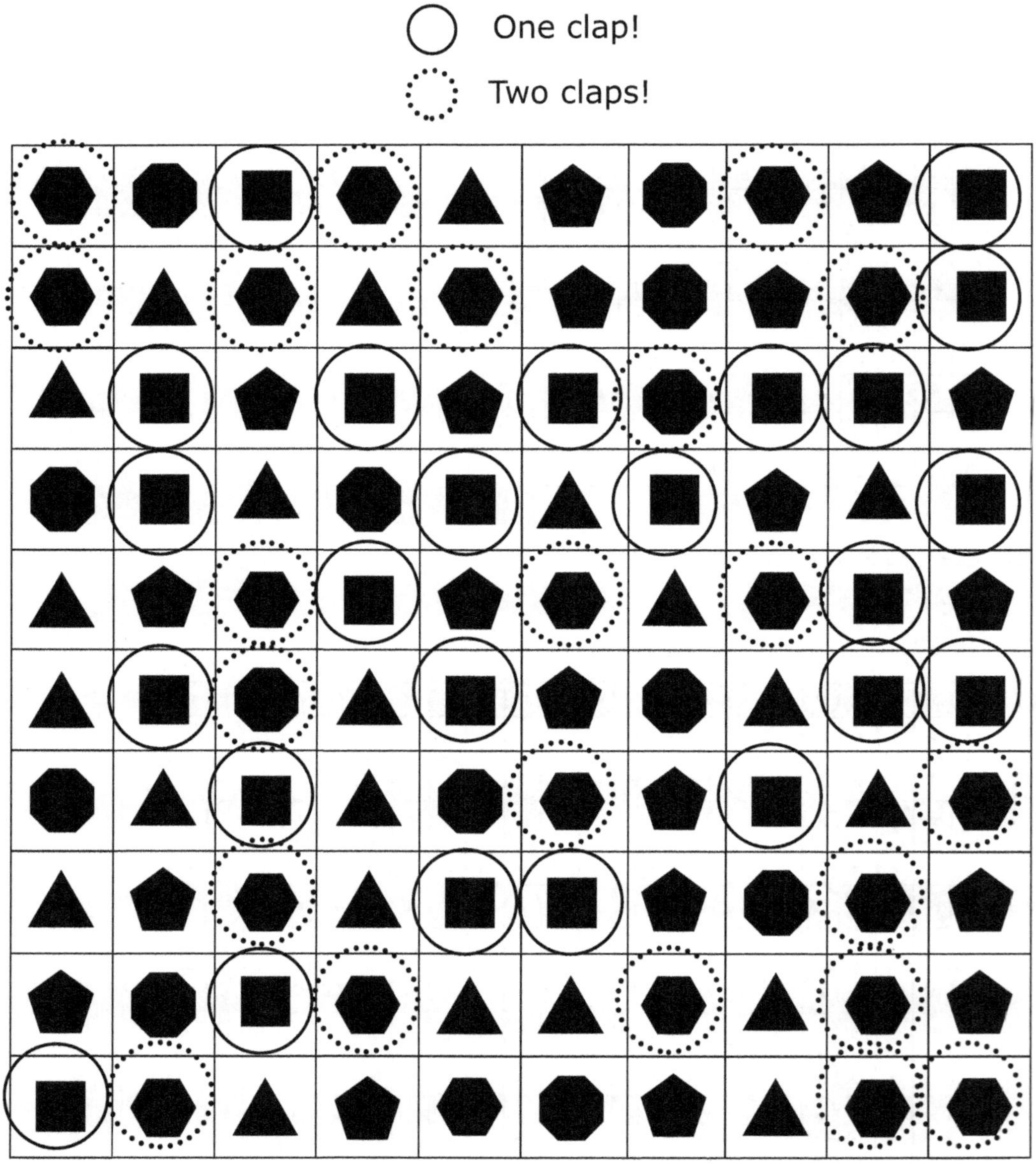

(e) Exercise 5: Attention ping-pong

- Ages: 7–8 years old. The second exercise I propose, which is for younger children, would be for 5–6-year olds.
- Solution:

	Left column	Right column
1	③9 7 2 8	8 7 2④9
2	W I Ⓑ P X	W P X I Ⓐ
3	C 4①T E	4 E C T⑧
4	9 8 3⑤4 6	6 9②3 8 4
5	R Ⓝ B L U A	L B R U A Ⓖ
6	9 S 2①8⑦	8 9 Ⓘ 2 Ⓜ S
7	⑧7 1 4⑤6 2	6⑨2③1 4 7
8	X J Ⓐ W B Ⓕ Ⓤ D	Ⓥ Ⓢ X Ⓟ J B D W

Left column	Right column

(f) Exercise 6: Prize for the most attentive

- Ages: 6–7
- Solution:

  How many words were there in total? 10 words.

  Do you remember if any words contained the letter H? Yes, one (vehicle).

Was there a verb among the words? No, no verb.

Did the word truck appear? No, although van and vehicle did. And the last question, did we name any cities? Yes, Alicante.

(g) Exercise 7: Abracadabra

- Ages: 7–8
- Solution:

T	A	X↑	G
X	A	D	A
X↑	L	X	A
X↑	Z	Y	X
A	P	A	X↑
A	X↑	A	Q
X	R	A	C
A	X↑	S	J
A	X↑	B	A
X↑	R	A	X↑

(h) Exercise 8: Letter salad

- Ages: 5–6
- Solution:

b Red	q Green	d Blue	p Yellow	q Green	d Blue	p Yellow	b Red	q Green	p Yellow
q Green	d Blue	p Yellow	b Red	b Red	q Green	d Blue	p Yellow	q Green	p Yellow
d Blue	p Yellow	q Green	b Red	b Red	p Yellow	q Green	d Blue	p Yellow	b Red
p Yellow	d Blue	b Red	q Green	d Blue	p Yellow	d Blue	p Yellow	b Red	b Red
d Blue	p Yellow	b Red	b Red	p Yellow	q Green	d Blue	p Yellow	q Green	b Red

p Yellow	d Blue	d Blue	b Red	q Green	d Blue	p Yellow	q Green	p Yellow	b Red
q Green	d Blue	p Yellow	b Red	d Blue	q Green	d Blue	p Yellow	q Green	b Red
p Yellow	q Green	d Blue	p Yellow	b Red	b Red	q Green	d Blue	p Yellow	q Green
d Blue	p Yellow	q Green	b Red	d Blue	p Yellow	d Blue	p Yellow	b Red	b Red
b Red	q Green	d Blue	p Yellow	q Green	d Blue	p Yellow	b Red	p Yellow	d Blue

Red = b	Blue = d	Yellow = p	Green = q

(i) Exercise 9: Orange juice

- Ages: 6–7
- Solution:

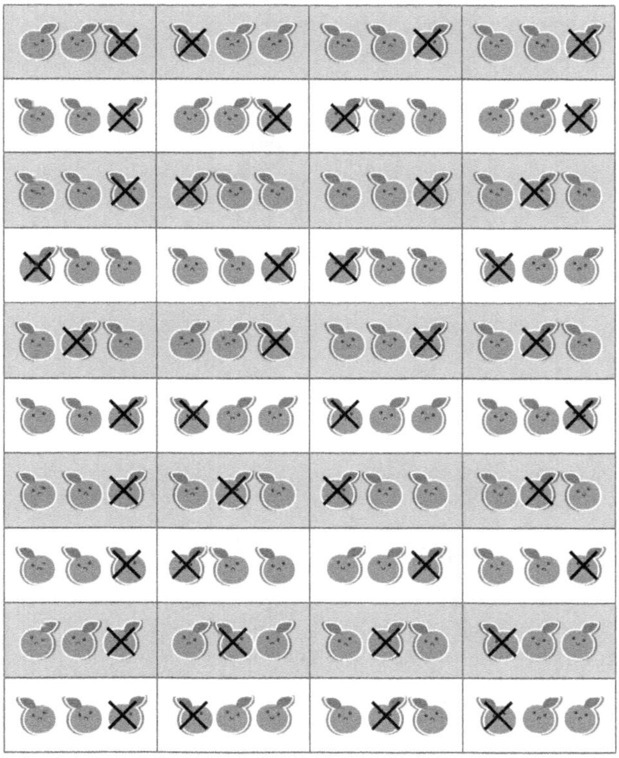

(j) Exercise 10: Find and compare

- Ages: 4–5
- Solution:

(ii) Chapter 6: Exercises to develop impulse control

(a) Exercise 1: Animal Stroop

- Ages: 6–7 years
- Solution:

Task 1:

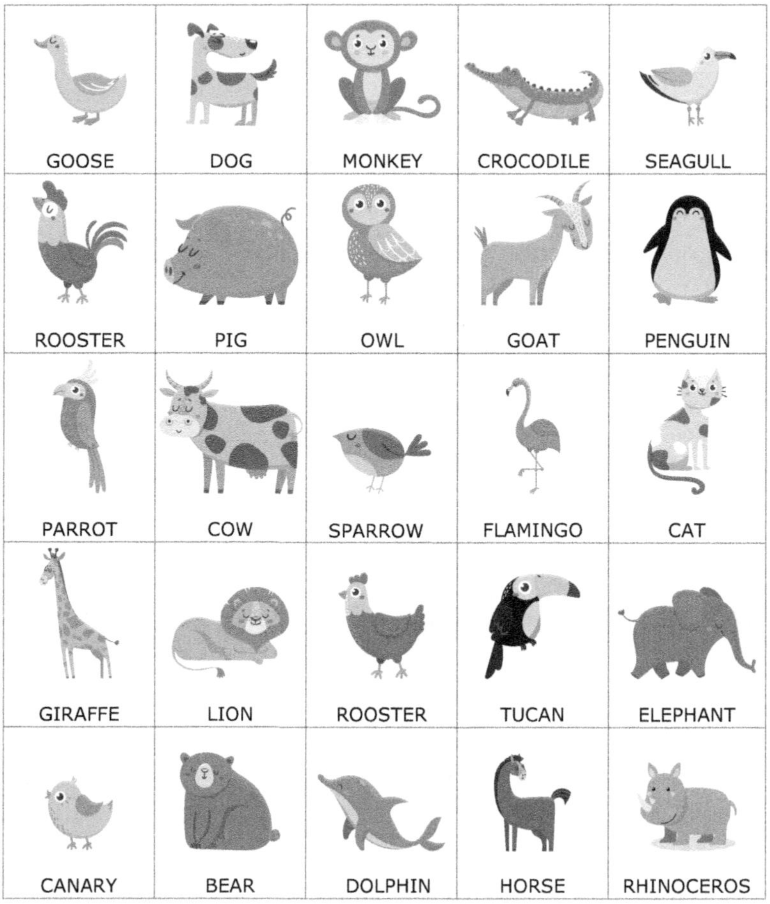

Task 2:

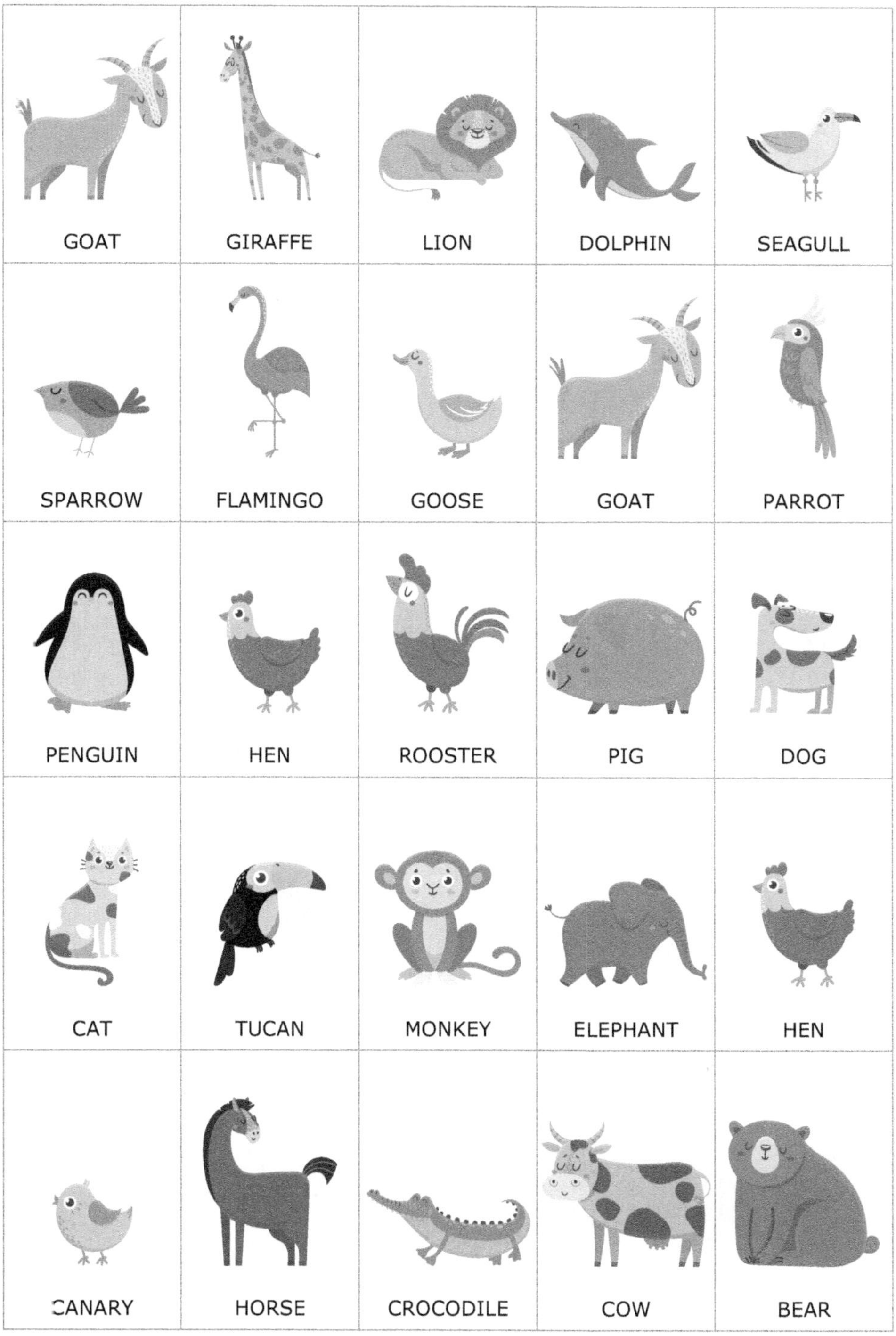
GOAT
GIRAFFE
LION
DOLPHIN
SEAGULL
SPARROW
FLAMINGO
GOOSE
GOAT
PARROT
PENGUIN
HEN
ROOSTER
PIG
DOG
CAT
TUCAN
MONKEY
ELEPHANT
HEN
CANARY
HORSE
CROCODILE
COW
BEAR

Task 3:

 OCA	 DOG	 MONKEY	 CROCODILE	 SEAGULL
 ROOSTER	 PIG	 OWL	 GOAT	 PENGUIN
 PARROT	 COW	 SPARROW	 FLAMINGO	 CAT
 GIRAFFE	 LION	 HEN	 TUCAN	 ELEPHANT
 TUCAN	 BEAR	 DOLPHIN	 HORSE	 RHINOCEROS

(b) Exercise 2: Everyone says yes

- Ages: 5–6
- Solution:

Yes	~~Yes*~~	Yes*	Yes
~~Yes*~~	~~Yes*~~	Yes	Yes
Yes	~~Yes*~~	~~Yes*~~	~~Yes*~~
Yes	~~Yes*~~	Yes	Yes
Yes	Yes	~~Yes*~~	Yes
~~Yes*~~	~~Yes*~~	Yes	~~Yes*~~
Yes	~~Yes*~~	Yes	~~Yes*~~

(c) Exercise 3: Detective González

- Ages: The first task is for children aged 4–5, and the second is for children aged 6–7
- Solution:

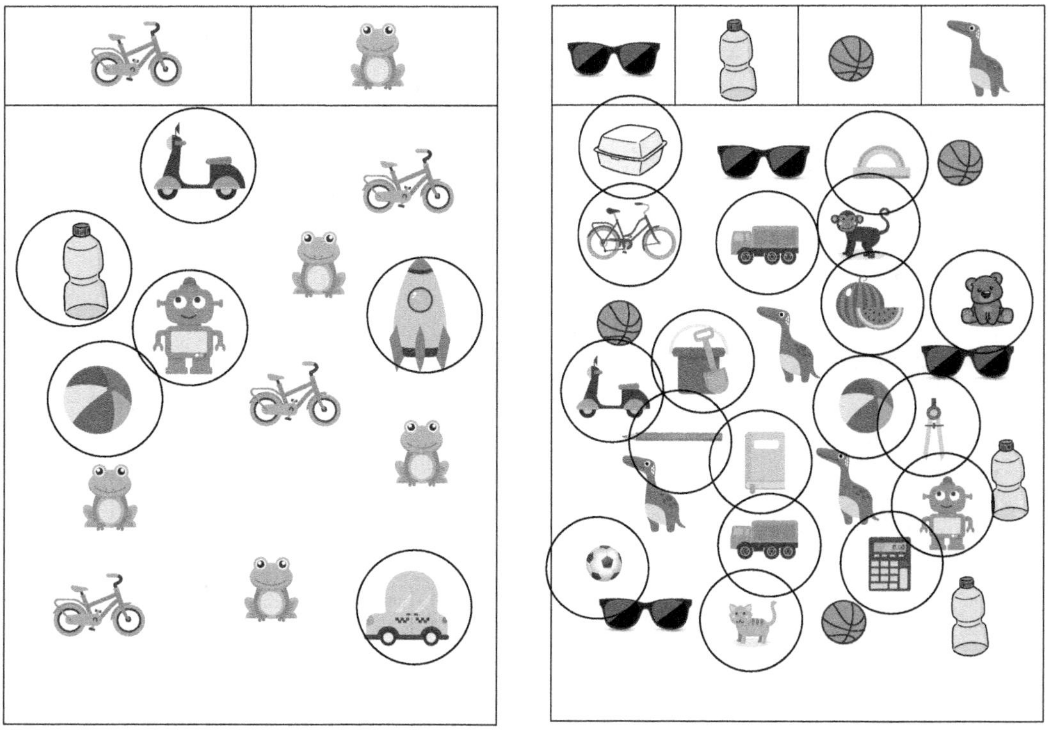

(d) Exercise 4: Playing with numbers

- Ages: 8–9
- Solution:

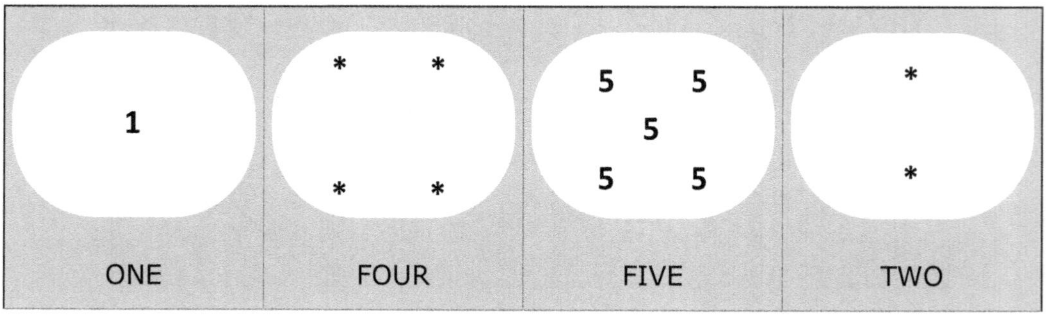

4 4 4 4 FOUR	5 5 5 5 5 FIVE	* * TWO	3 3 3 THREE
* * * THREE	* * * * FOUR	1 ONE	* * * * * FIVE
3 3 3 THREE	2 2 TWO	5 5 5 5 5 FIVE	* ONE
1 1 TWO	* * TWO	4 FOUR	* * * THREE
4 4 FOUR	* ONE	* * * THREE	* ONE

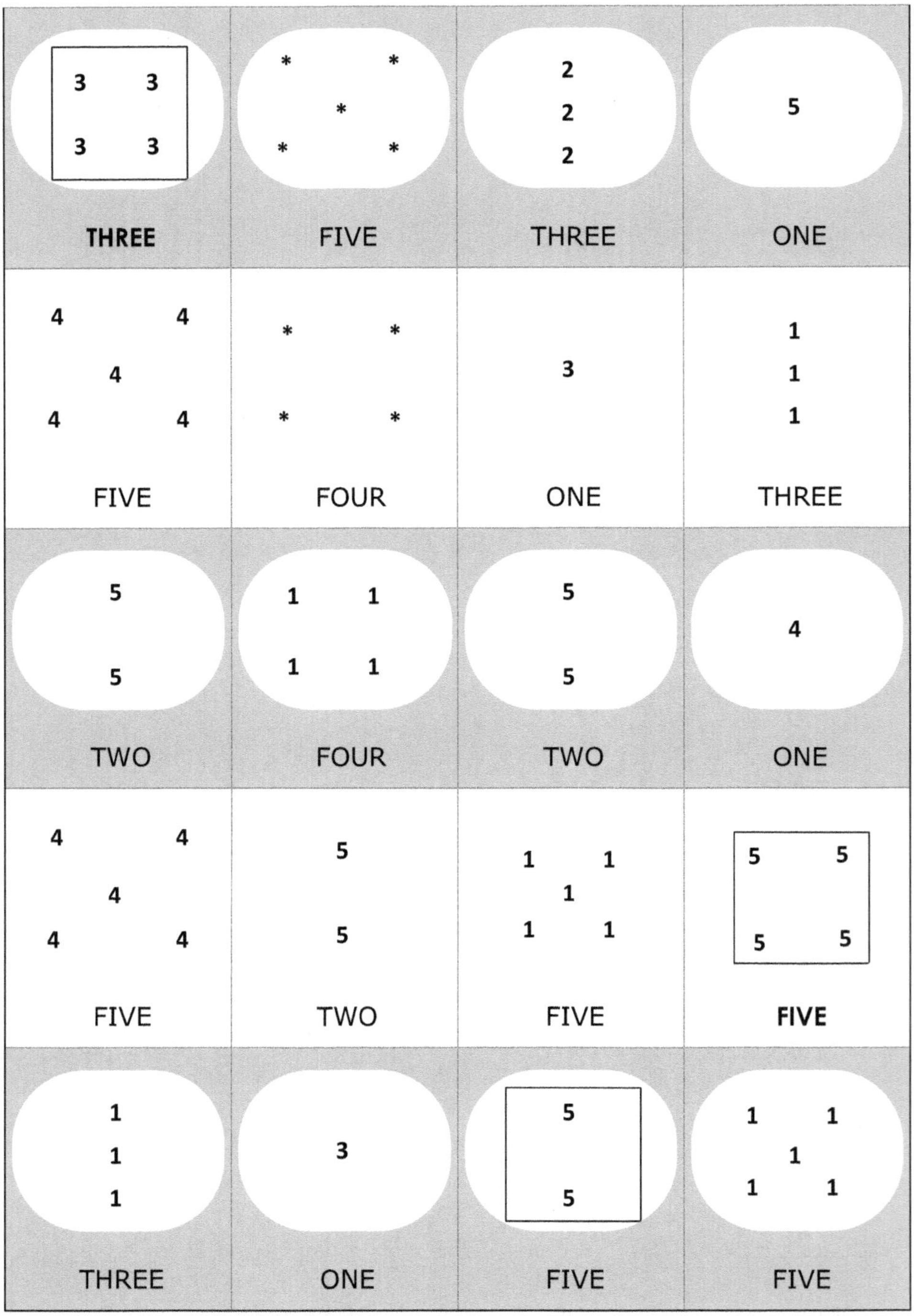
3 3 3 3
THREE
* * * * *
FIVE
2 2 2
THREE
5
ONE
4 4 4 4 4
FIVE
* * * *
FOUR
3
ONE
1 1 1
THREE
5 5
TWO
1 1 1 1
FOUR
5 5
TWO
4
ONE
4 4 4 4 4
FIVE
5 5
TWO
1 1 1 1 1
FIVE
5 5 5 5
FIVE
1 1 1
THREE
3
ONE
5 5
FIVE
1 1 1 1 1
FIVE

(e) Exercise 5: One step forward

- Ages: 6–7
- Solution:

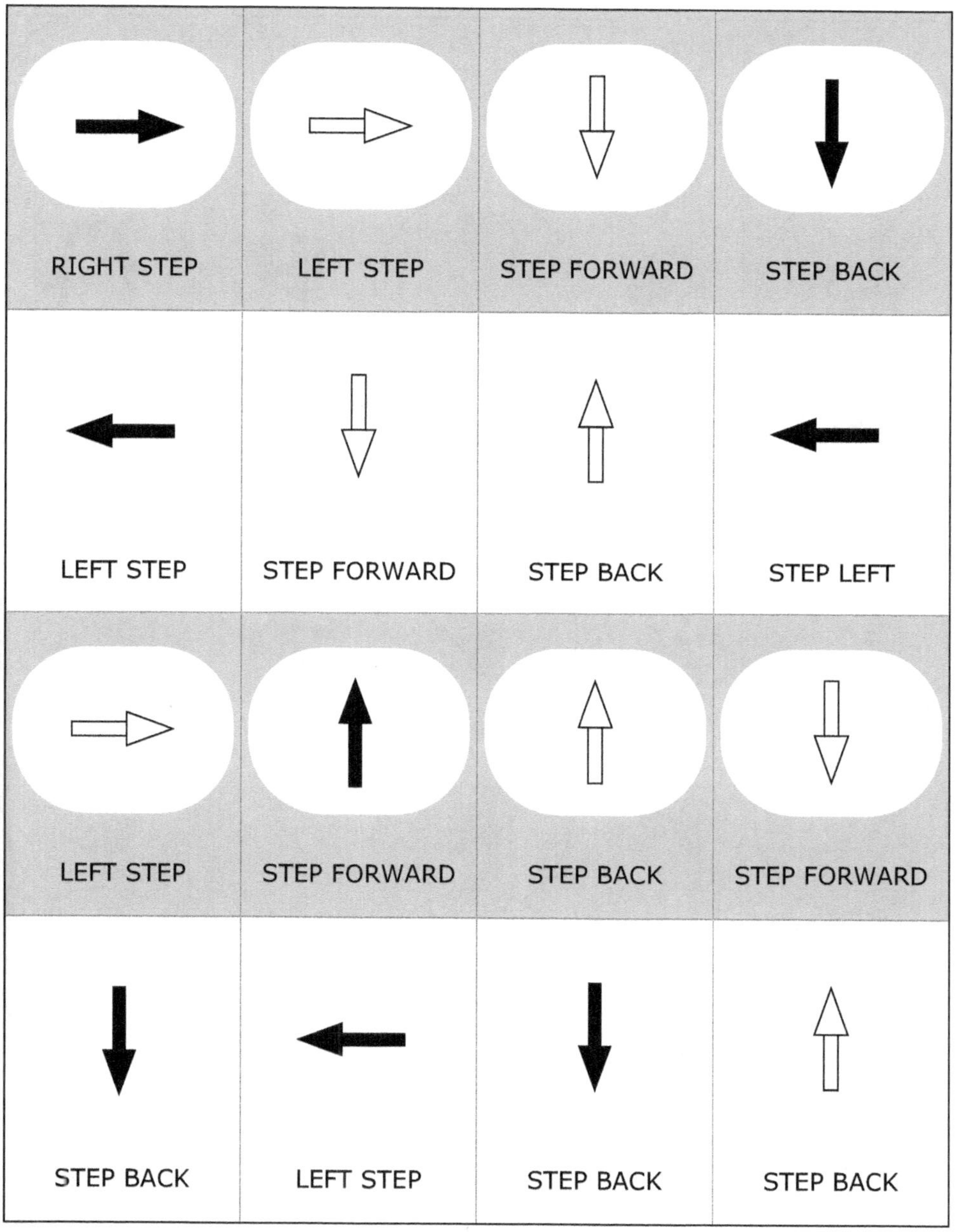

(f) Exercise 6: A walk around the zoo

- Ages: 6–7
- Solution:

(g) Exercise 7: Sneakers and hands

- Ages: 6–7
- Solution:

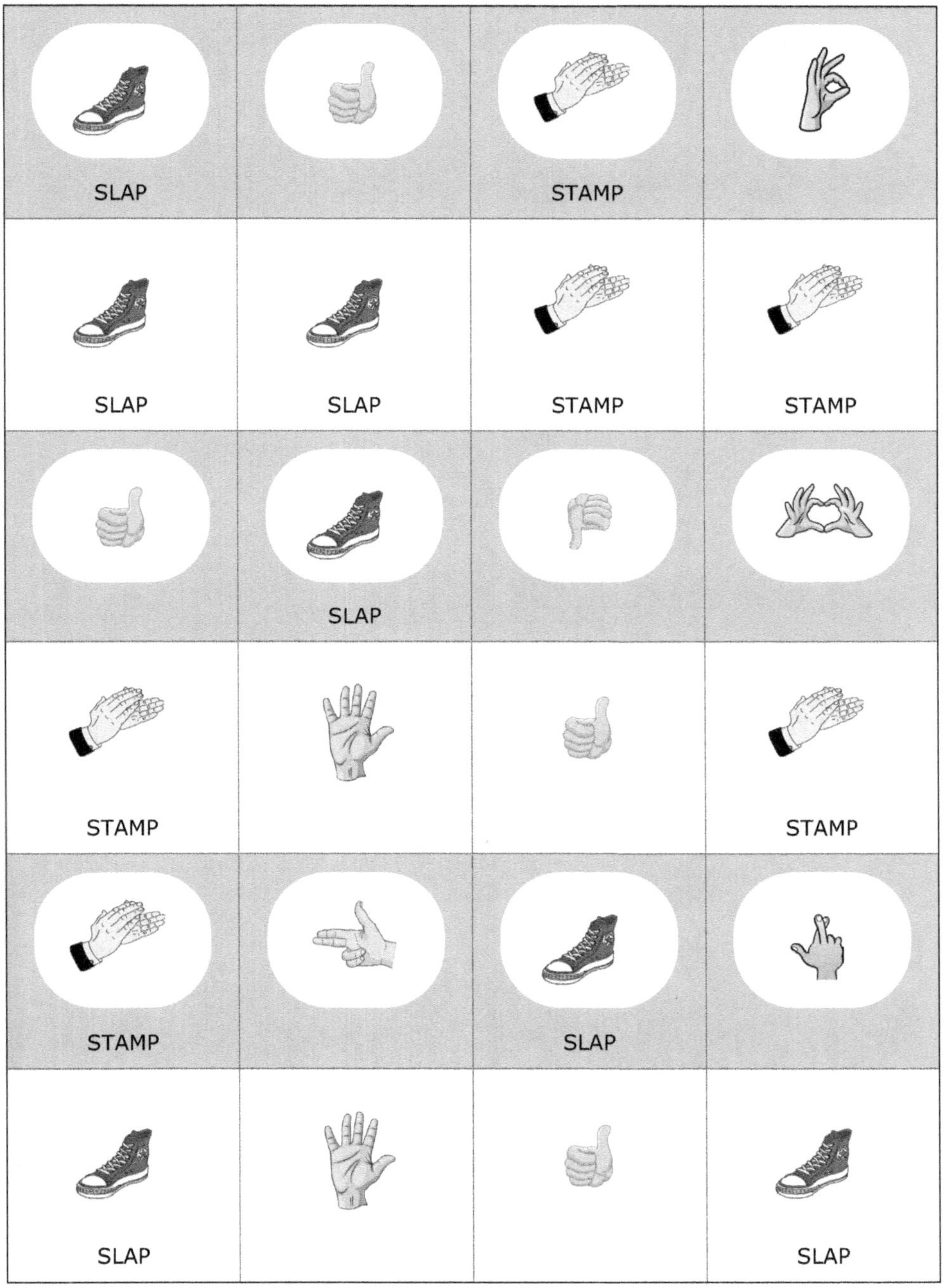

(h) Exercise 8: Moon and sun

- Ages: 3–4
- Solution:

(i) ***Exercise 9: Watch out for number 2!***

- Ages: 6–7
- Solution:

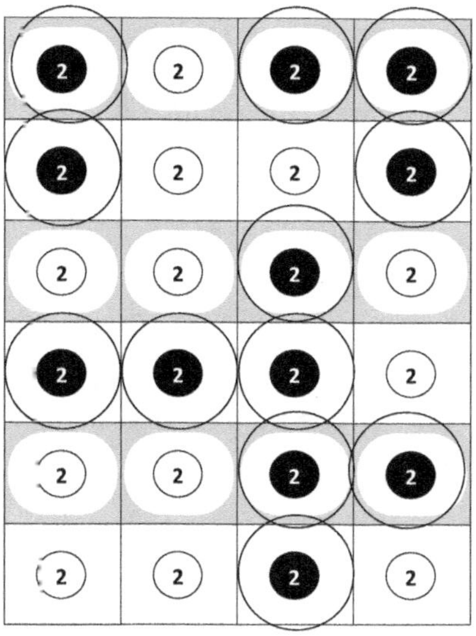

(i) ***Exercise 10: The nosy windows***

- Ages: 7–8
- Solution:

(iii) Chapter 7: Exercises to develop working memory

(a) Exercise 1: Number dance

- Ages: 7–8
- Solution:
  → Form the lowest number: 23479.
  → Form three even numbers: There are several correct answers, for example, 92374, 72394, and 43792.
  → Form the highest possible number: 97432.
  → Form all possible 5-digit numbers that start with 3 and end with 9: 32479, 32749, 34279, 34729, 37249, and 37429.

(b) Exercise 2: Nicolás the crab

- Ages: As this is an exercise of increasing difficulty, it can be done from the age of 4 onwards and is also suitable and interesting for teenagers and adults.
- Solution:
  2 elements: 7-5 / 1-4
  3 Elements: 8-1-5 / 6-3-9
  4 elements: 8-1-7-3 / 6-2-9-5
  5 elements: 9-5-8-2-4 / 2-1-6-4-9
  6 elements: 9-1-8-4-2-6 / 9-5-6-1-4-3

(c) Exercise 3: Counting euros

- Ages: 6–7 years
- Solution: Laura has 7 euros, Luis has 5 euros, Julia has 4 euros, Miguel has 7 euros, Susana has 7 euros, and Jonás has 6 euros.

(d) Exercise 4: The human calculator

- Ages: 9–10
- Solution:

  a 6.
  b It's the same, both give 5.
  c 32 horses x 4 legs each = 128 legs in total.
  d 24 times in one day.
  e 1,050 seconds.
  f 123 days.
  g 12.
  h 7 eyes.

(e) Exercise 5: Sudoku

- Ages: First sudoku (7 years old) and second sudoku (10 years old and up)
- Solution:

4	2	1	3
3	1	4	2
2	4	3	1
1	3	2	4

2	3	6	8	5	1	4	7	9
1	5	4	2	7	9	6	3	8
8	7	9	6	3	4	1	5	2
7	9	5	3	1	8	2	4	6
3	8	2	4	9	6	7	1	5
4	6	1	5	2	7	8	9	3
5	4	7	9	6	2	3	8	1
9	2	8	1	4	3	5	6	7
6	1	3	7	8	5	9	2	4

(f) Exercise 6: King Kong

- Ages: 8–9
- Solution:

6 10 **5 10** 18 **1 2 4** 9 7 16 **8 16** **3 6 12** 1 3 5 11 4

(g) Exercise 7: Crazy numbers

- Ages 7–8
- Solution:

10	+	3	=	13
-		-		-
2	+	1	=	3
=		=		=
8	+	2	=	10

8	-	3	=	5
+		+		+
6	-	4	=	2
=		=		=
14	-	7	=	7

10	+	14	=	24
-		-		-
2	+	13	=	15
=		=		=
8	+	1	=	9

26	-	17	=	9
+		+		+
7	-	5	=	2
=		=		=
33	-	22	=	11

(h) Exercise 8: Thinking about numbers

- Ages: 7–8
- Solution: 34 (adding 2 and subtracting 3): 36, 33, 35, 32, 34, 31, 33, 30, 32, 29, 31, 28, 30, 27, 29, 26, 28, 25, 27, 24, 26, 23, 25, 22, 24, 21, 23, 25, 22, 24; 21, 23, 20, 22, 19, 21, 18, 20, 17, 19, 16, 18, 15, 17, 14, 16, 13, 15, 12, 14, 11, 13, 10, 12, 9, 11, 8, 10, 7, 9, 6, 8, 5, 7, 4, 6, 3, 5, 2, 4, 1, 3, 0.

(i) Exercise 9: Card memory

- Ages: 3 and up
- Solution: The player who finds the most pairs of cards wins the game.

(j) Exercise 10: Use your mental dictionary

- Ages: 8–9
- Solution:

  Cologne - Game
  Wardrobe - Horse
  Bedroom - Tomato - Frog
  Eggplant - Heat - Humidity
  Water - Case - Computer - Hair
  Basketball - Basket - Skiing - Ball - Racket
  Pen - Oven - Pencil - Mallow - Goal - Pipe

(iv) Chapter 8: Exercises to develop cognitive flexibility

(a) Exercise 1: Pull everything you can think of out of a hat

- Ages: 3–4 years and up
- Solution: Let your imagination run wild!

(b) Exercise 2: The matchstick bull

- Ages: 5–6 years
- Solution:

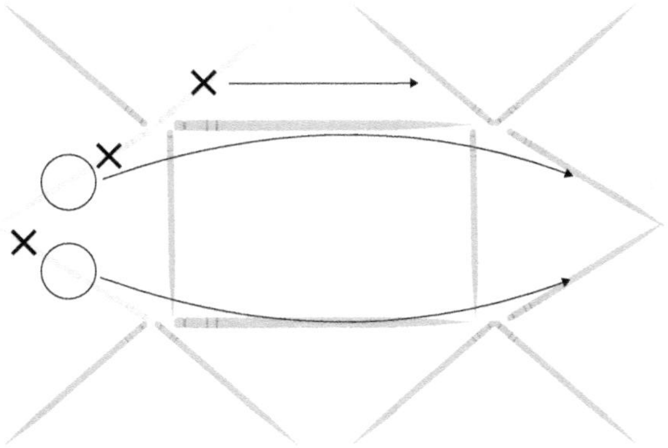

(c) Exercise 3: The magic triangle

- Ages: 5–6
- Solution:

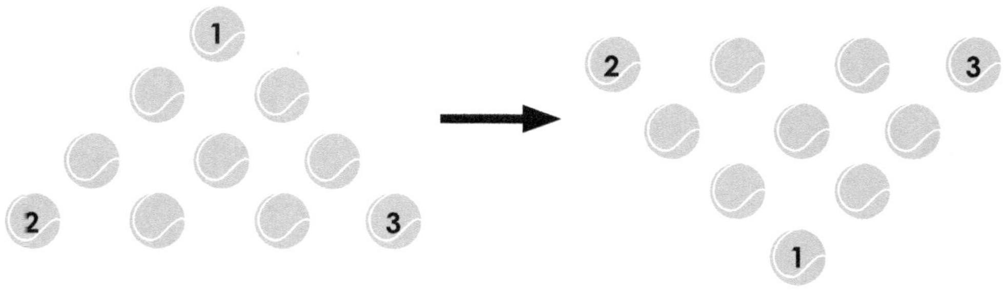

(d) Exercise 4: The five dots

- Ages: 5–6
- Solution: Here are some of the solutions

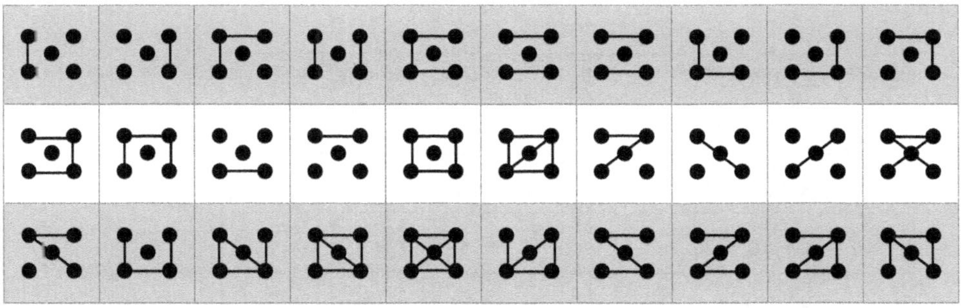

(e) Exercise 5: Matchsticks and numbers

- Ages 7–8
- Solution:

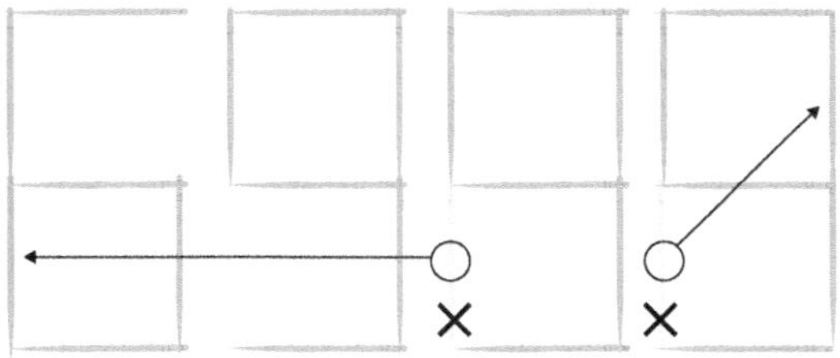

(f) Exercise 6: All the words

- Ages: From 5 years old, depending on the difficulty
- Solution: Let your imagination run wild!

(g) Exercise 7: Four straight lines

- Ages: 9–10 years and up
- Solution:

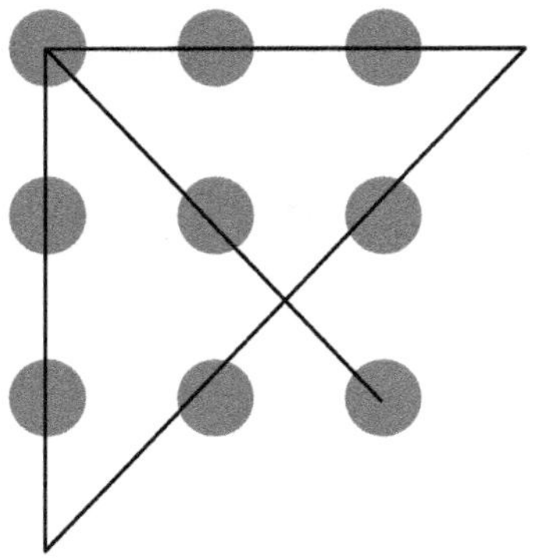

(h) Exercise 8: Addition and subtraction

- Ages: 7 and up
- Solution:

ADDITION	SUBTRACTION
6 + 13 = 19	17 –12 = 5
16 + 26 = 42	23 –3 –4 = 16
7 + 3 + 19 = 29	42 –17 = 25
23 + 12 = 35	34 – 21 = 13
3 + 4 + 7 = 14	54 – 27 = 27
11 + 18 + 23 = 52	14 –3 – 5 = 6
4 + 56 + 21 = 81	34 – 13 = 21
19 + 23 = 42	32 – 21 – 3 = 8
45 + 23 = 68	45 – 32 = 13
65 + 21 + 34 = 120	11 – 7 – 1 = 3
66 + 21 + 2 = 89	65 – 3 – 22 = 40

(i) Exercise 9: Finding Nemo

- Ages: 7–8
- Solution:

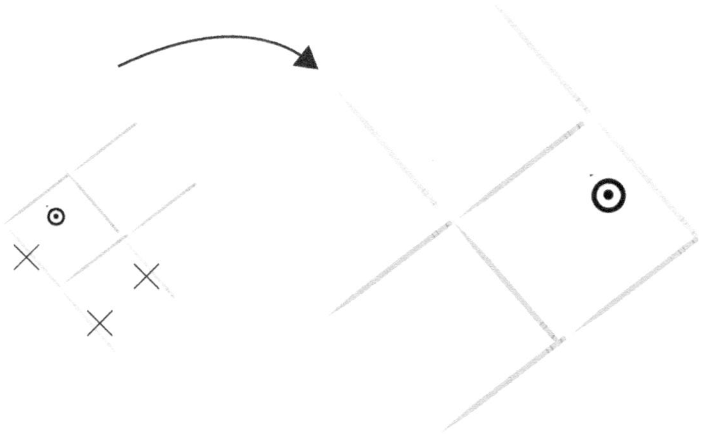

(j) Exercise 10: Picasso's abstraction

- Ages: 6
- Solution: There are endless solutions to this exercise. That is why we are giving you some examples of the many correct answers that exist.

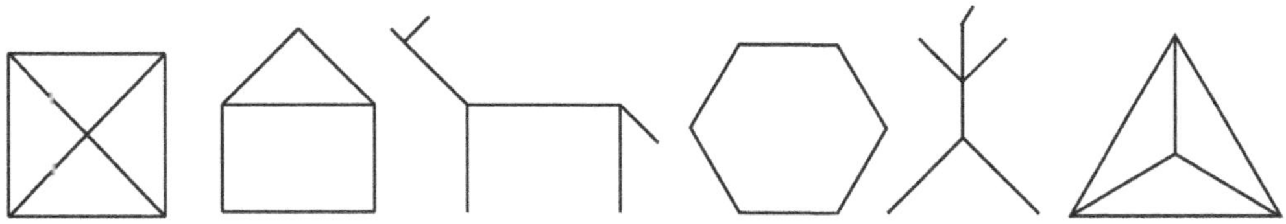

(v) Chapter 9: Exercises to develop planning skills

(a) Exercise 1: What a mess!

- Ages: 5–6
- Solution:

(b) Exercise 2: Tower of Hanoi

- Ages: 6 and up
- Solution: To complete the simplest task in the Tower of Hanoi (3 discs) with the fewest number of moves, the discs would have to be moved as follows:

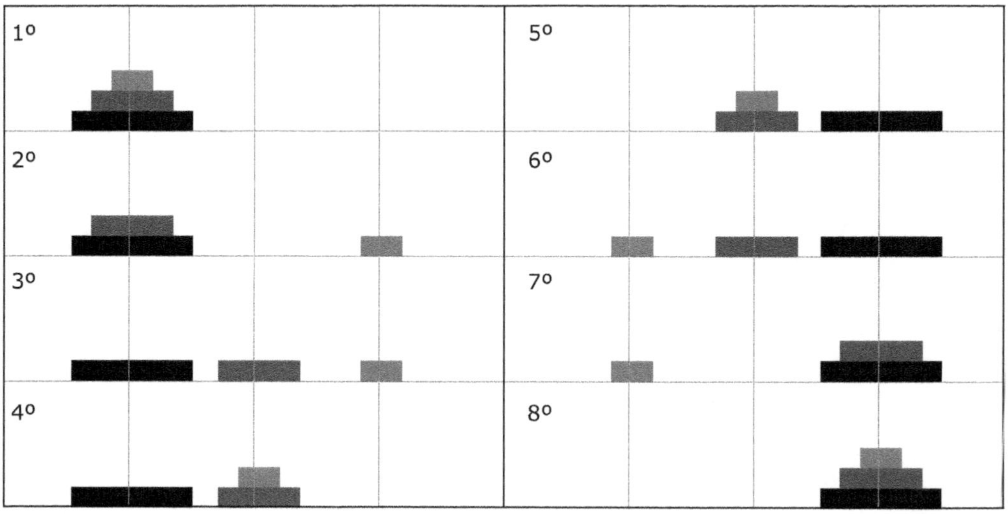

(c) Exercise 3: Crazy numbers

- Ages: 6–7 years and up
- Solution: As there are three exercises in ascending order of difficulty, here are their solutions:

1 1, 3, 5, 6, 7, 8, 9, 10, 12, 32, and 40.
2 1, 2, 3, 5, 7, 8, 10, 12, 13, 14, 21, 24, 25, and 33.
3 87, 55, 45, 33, 22, 17, 14, 9, 4, 3, and 0.

(d) Exercise 4: The French omelet

- Ages: 5–6
- Solution:

1 Hold the eggs.
2 Crack the eggs.
3 Add a pinch of salt.
4 Beat the eggs.
5 Heat the oil.
6 Pour the eggs into the pan.
7 Flip the omelet.
8 Serve the omelet on a plate.

(e) Exercise 5: Mazes

- Ages: Depending on the mazes, from 4 to 5 years old
- Solution:

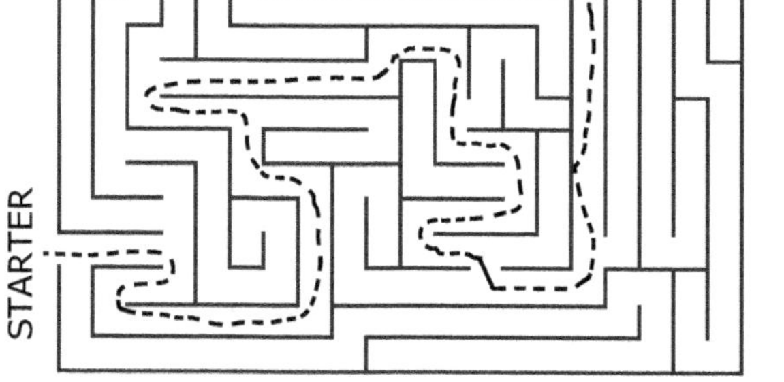

(f) Exercise 6: Connecting the dots

- Ages: 4–5 years and up
- Solution:

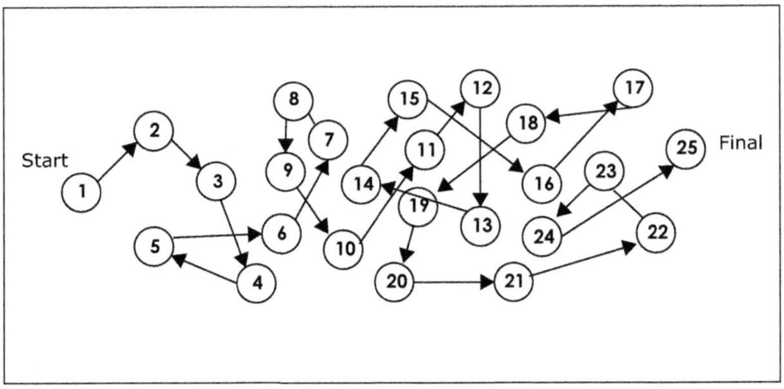

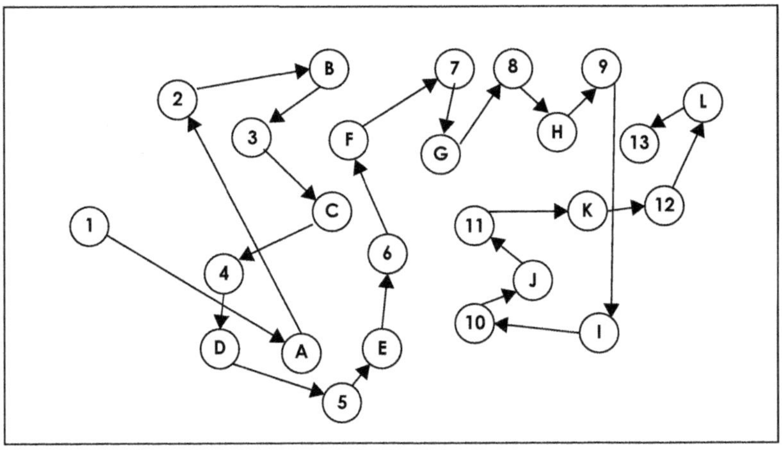

(g) Exercise 7: Cats and dogs

- Ages: 7–8
- Solution:

1 A cat and a dog must leave; the dog stays on shore 2.
2 The cat returns and takes another dog to shore 2.
3 Once again, the cat returns and takes another cat, leaves it, and brings one of the dogs that was on shore 2 back to shore 1.
4 It takes the last cat and sends the only dog left on shore 2 back to bring another dog.
5 Once again, the dog returns to shore 1 to bring the last dog.

(h) Exercise 8: The crazy dictionary

- Ages: 5–6
- Solution:

Tools: hammer, screwdriver, nail, drill, pliers, wrench, hammer, and screw.
Foods: chickpeas, strawberries, hake, bread, eggs, beans, and monkfish.
Animals: lion, ant, dog, and bear.

(i) Exercise 9: Number tutti-frutti

- Ages: 6–7
- Solution:

Name all the even numbers: 12 and 32.
Order the odd numbers from smallest to largest: 1, 5, 9, 13, 23, 41, 57, and 89.
Order the even numbers from largest to smallest: 32 and 12.
Order the numbers greater than 10 and less than 50 from smallest to largest: 12, 13, 23, 32, and 41.

(j) Exercise 10: The king of symbols

- Ages: 6–7
- Solution:

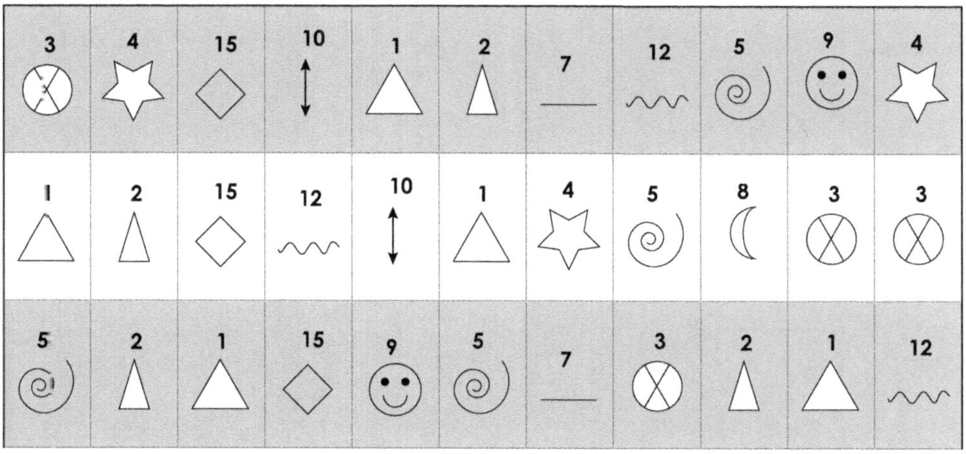

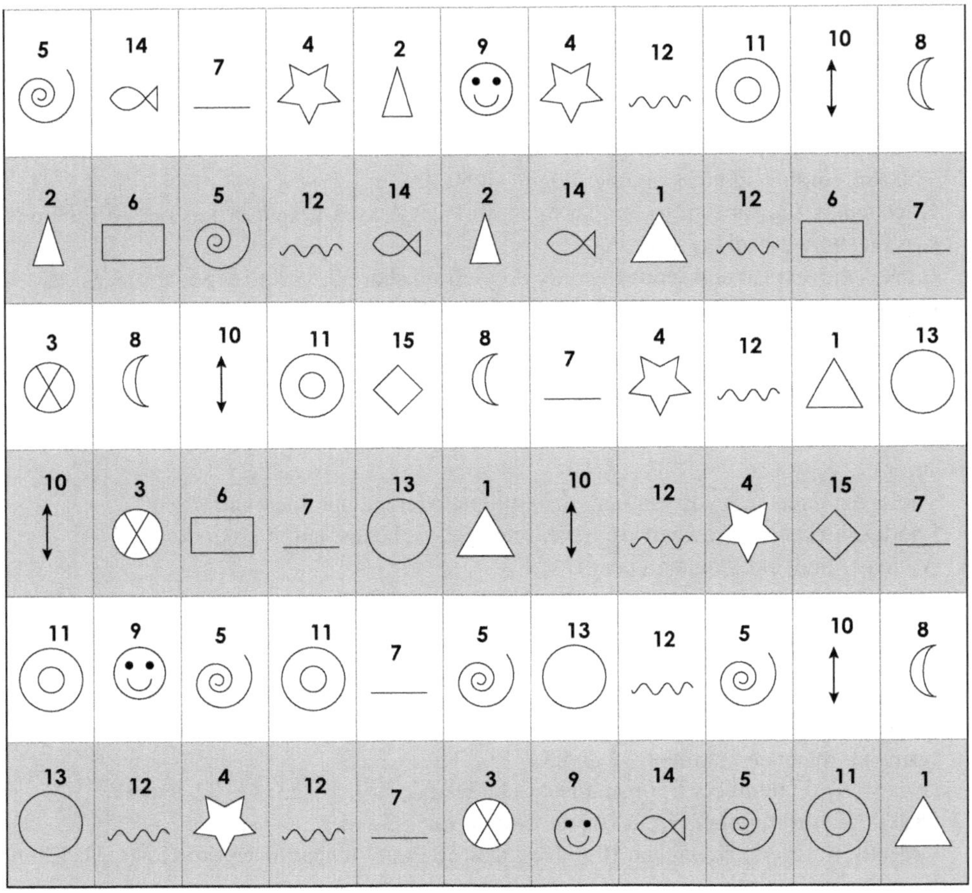

(vi) Chapter 10: Exercises to develop problem-solving skills

(a) Exercise 1: The little house

- Ages: 5–6
- Solution:

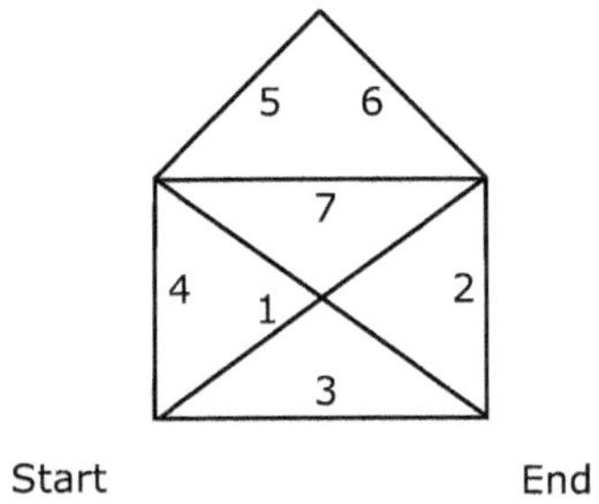

(b) Exercise 2: Hunting mice

- Ages: 5–6
- Solution: 5 cats

(c) Exercise 3: The hourglasses

- Ages: 7–8
- Solution:

How can we measure exactly 15 minutes if we only have two hourglasses, one lasting 11 minutes and the other 7 minutes?

Solution

Start both timers at the same time. When the 7-minute timer goes off, place the pan on the stove. The 11-minute timer will have 4 minutes left to go. As soon as those 4 minutes are up, turn it over again, so that the 4 minutes plus the 11 minutes add up to the 15 minutes needed to cook the rice.

When the 11-minute hourglass runs out, 11 minutes will have passed, and 4 minutes will have passed in the 7-minute hourglass. If the 7-minute hourglass is turned over at that moment, it will have sand for 4 minutes, which added to the 11 minutes that have already passed makes a total of 15 minutes.

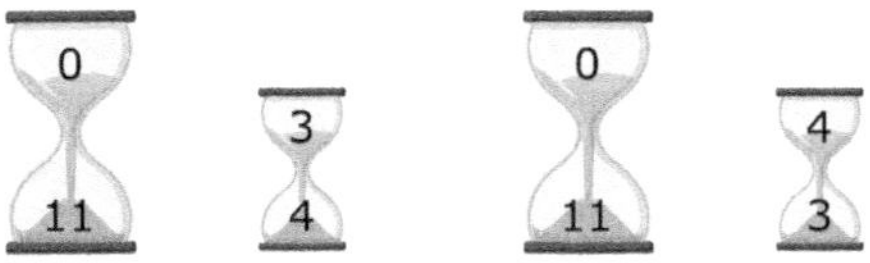

(d) Exercise 4: Nineland

- Ages: 11–12
- Solution:

  The smallest number of coins needed to pay the 6351 florins is 21 coins:
  6 coins worth 1 florin.
  6 coins worth 9 florins.

3 coins worth 99 florins.
6 coins of 999 florins.
$6 \times 1 + 6 \times 9 + 3 \times 99 + 6 \times 999 = 6351$ florins

(e) *Exercise 5: The ages*

- Ages: 7–8 years
- Solution:

Antonio (the youngest of the brothers) is 15 years old, Juan (the middle brother) is 20 years old, and the oldest (Francisco) is 35 years old.

20 - 15 = 5 years (the age difference between Juan and Antonio).

35 = 15 + 20 (the age of the oldest child is equal to the sum of the ages of the middle and youngest children).

15 + 20 + 35 = 70 (the sum of the brothers' ages is equal to 70).

(f) *Exercise 6: The candy boxes*

- Ages: 12–13
- Solution:

You only need to take one piece of candy. The important thing is to take the first and only piece of candy from the box labeled "Mix." Since all the boxes are mislabeled, if we take a piece of candy from the box labeled "Mix," we will have two possible options:

→ Option 1: If the candy in the box labeled "Mezcla" is mint, then we know that this box must be the mint one; the one labeled "Men-ta" must be the anise one, and the anise one must be the "Mezcla" one (we conclude this because all the labels are wrong).
→ Option 2: If we get an anise candy from the box labeled "Mix," then the box labeled "Anise" will be mint, and the one labeled "Mint" will be "Mix."

(g) *Exercise 7: The chocolate cups*

- Ages: 10–11
- Solution:

Yes, it is possible to distribute the same amount of chocolate and cups among the three children.

Each child will receive the equivalent of 3 and a half cups of chocolate and a total of 7 cups as follows:

→ Child A: 2 glasses full of chocolate, 3 glasses half full, and 2 empty glasses.
→ Child B: 2 glasses full of chocolate, 3 glasses half full, and 2 empty glasses.
→ Child C: 3 glasses full of chocolate, 1 half full, and 3 empty.

(h) *Exercise 8: Letter addition*

- Ages: 12–13
- Solution:

T = 0 / G = 1 / O = 2 / B = 3 / A = 4 / D = 5 / N = 6 / R = 7 / L = 8 / E = 9

(i) *Exercise 9: The water fountain*

- Ages: 9–10
- Solution:

1. I fill the 5-liter container with water.
2. With the water I have in the 5-liter container, I fill the 3-liter container. As a result, I have 2 liters left in the 5-liter container (5 L – 3 L = 2 L).
3. I empty the 3-liter container.
4. I pour the 2 liters I have in the 5-liter container into the 3-liter container.
5. I refill the 5-liter jug at the fountain.
6. I pour the contents of the 5-liter container into the 3-liter one until it is full (I can only pour one liter, as I had 2 liters).
7. The remaining 4 liters from the 5-liter container will be the 4 liters they asked me for.

(j) *Exercise 10: Curious Jonás*

- Ages: 6–7
- Solution: The first missing tile is White-One, the second is Six-White, and the third is Three-White.

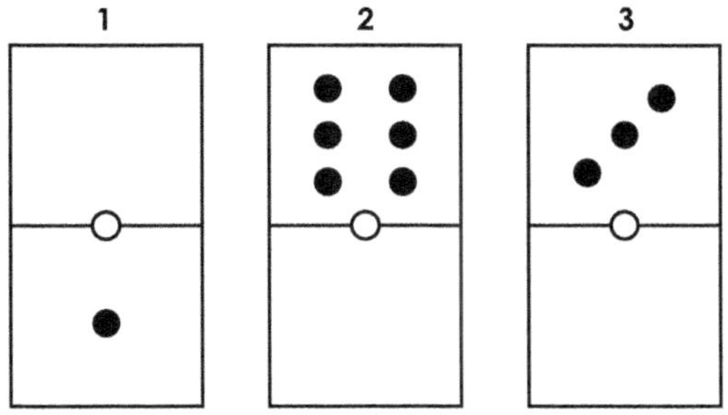

(vii) Chapter 11: Exercises to develop emotional self-regulation

There are no right or wrong answers here; these are exercises that I propose, but they do not have a single, definitive solution.

(viii) Chapter 12: Exercises to develop processing

(a) *Exercise 1: The Usain Bolt of words*

- Ages: Once the child has learned to read.
- Solution: Read the words as quickly as possible and pronounce them clearly.

(b) *Exercise 2: In search of the lost symbol*

- Ages: 5–6 years
- Solution:

(c) Exercise 3: Speed reading

- Ages: When the child has learned to read.
- Solution: There are no correct answers.

(d) Exercise 4: Naming objects

- Ages: 4–5
- Solution:

Dinosaur	Ball	Bottle	Magnifying glass	Motorcycle
Truck	Glasses	Paintbrush	Watermelon	Compass
Notebook	Bucket	Ball	Glue	T-shirt
Pencil	Apple	Penguin	Boat	Stuffed animal
Hat	Robot	Calculator	Airplane	Fish

(e) Exercise 5: Chess

- Ages: 5 and up
- Solution:

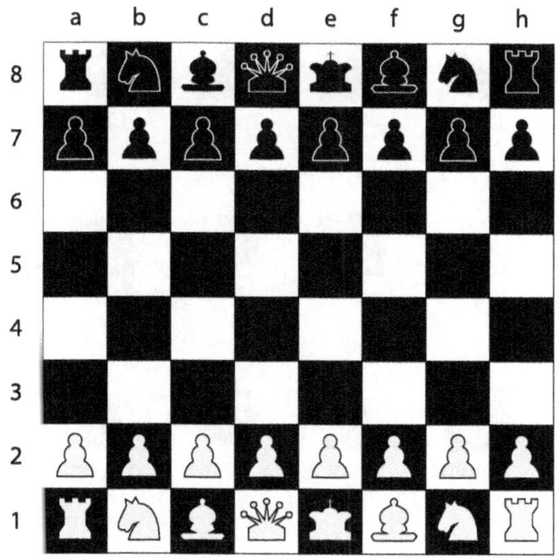

(f) Exercise 6: The Little Coachman, Leré

- Ages: 6–7
- Solution:

	CAR	
CAR	CHOCO	CHOCHE
COHCE	CAR	CAR
CAR	CAR	CECHO
CAR	CAR	CAR
OCHE	OCHE	COHCE
CHOCE	CAR	COHCE
CAR	CECHO	CAR
CAR	CAR	CECHO

(g) Exercise 7: The horse

- Ages: 4–5
- Solution: 16 horses

(h) Exercise 8: Geometric shape salad

- Ages: 4–5
- Solution:

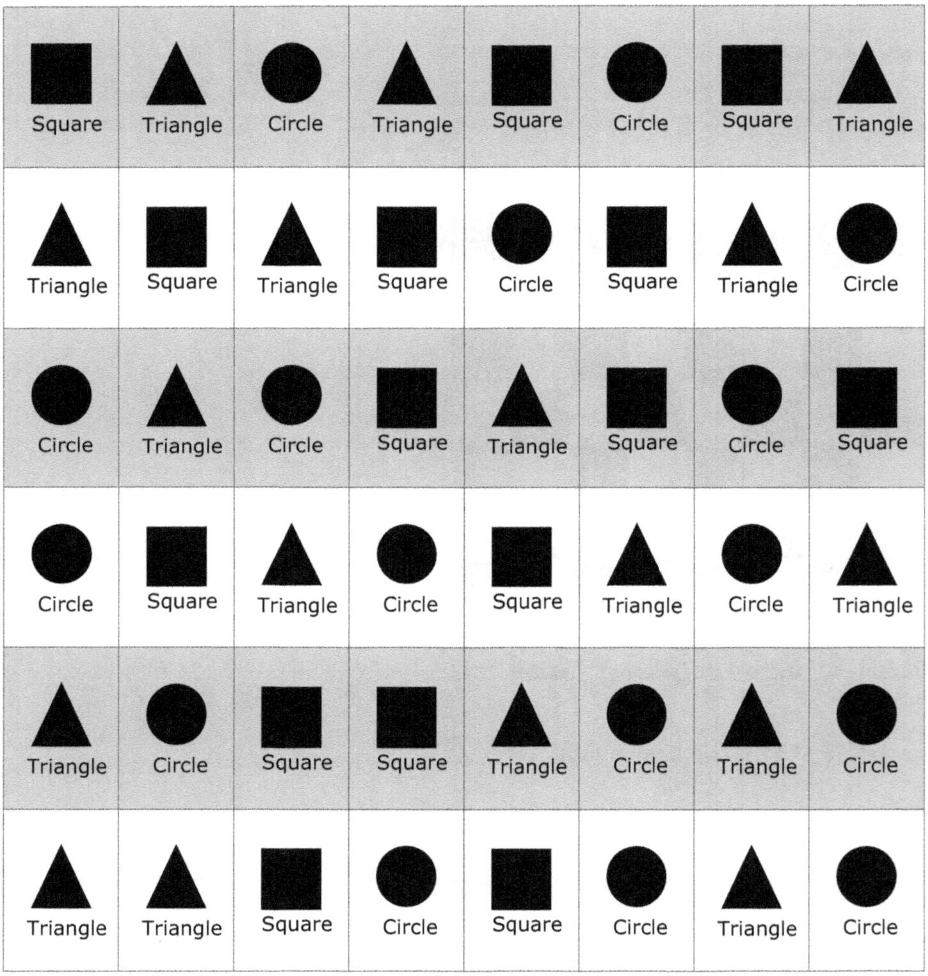

(i) Exercise 9: The body in motion

- Ages: Depending on the development of body awareness, this exercise can be done from ages 4–5 onwards.
- Solution: Carry out the task indicated in the exercise sufficiently well.

(j) Exercise 10: Completing the child figure

- Ages: 4–5 years
- Solution:

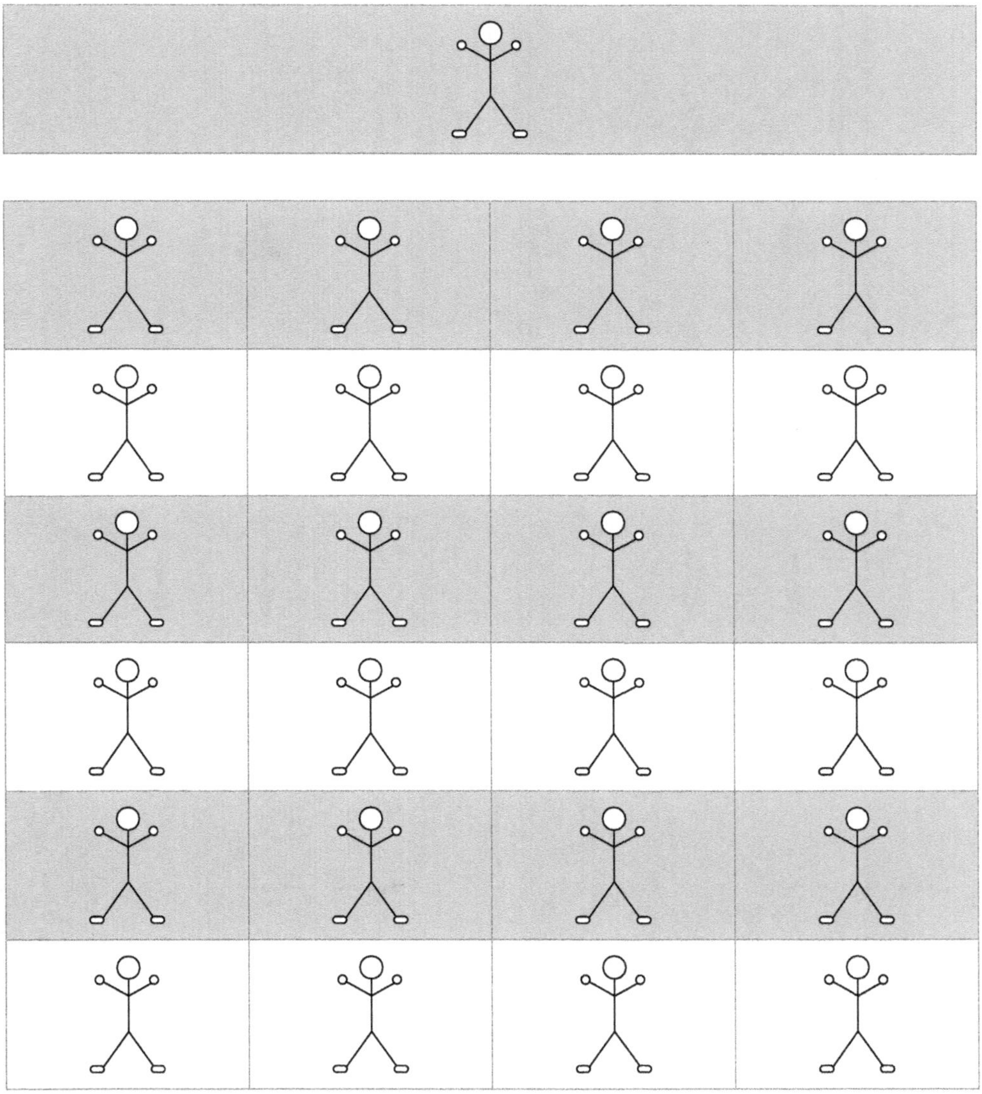

(ix) Chapter 13: Exercises to develop spatial orientation

(a) Exercise 1: The triangles

- Ages 4–5 years
- Solution:

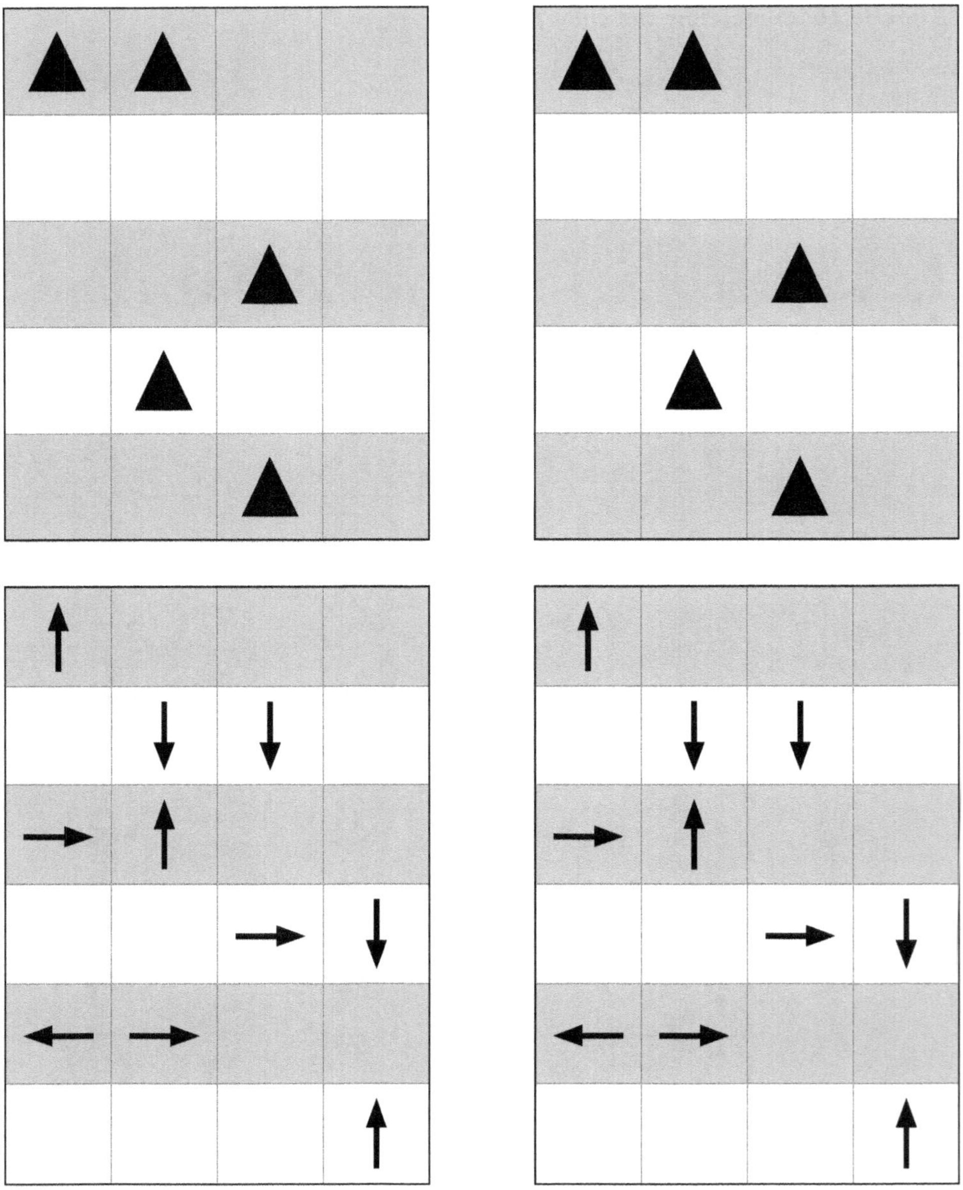

(b) Exercise 2: Get your body moving!

- Ages: From the moment they have developed their body schema (5–6 years and older)
- Solution: They should be able to carry out the instructions given in the exercise sufficiently well.

(c) Exercise 3: Copy, copy!

- Ages: 6–7 years
- Solution:

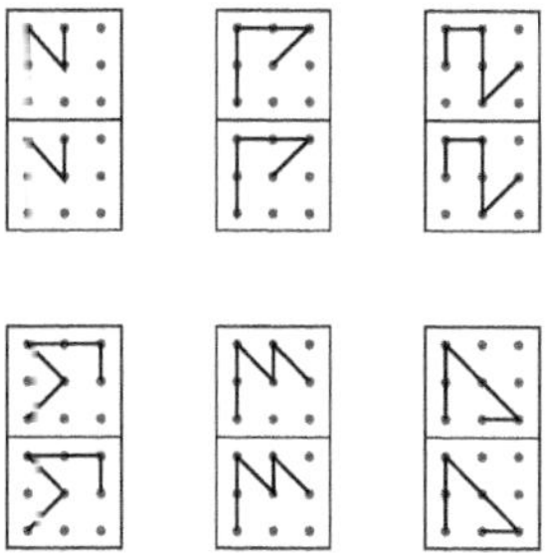

(d) Exercise 4: The backpack and the ball

- Ages: 4–5
- Solution:

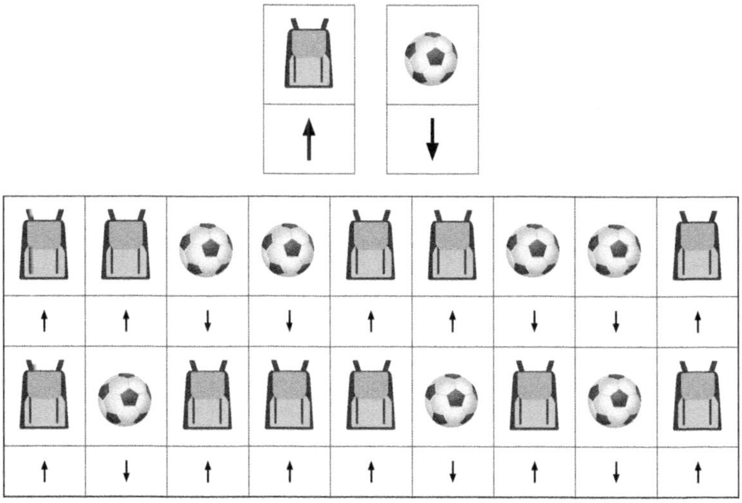

(e) Exercise 5: Which way are they going?

- Ages: 4–5 years and up
- Solution:

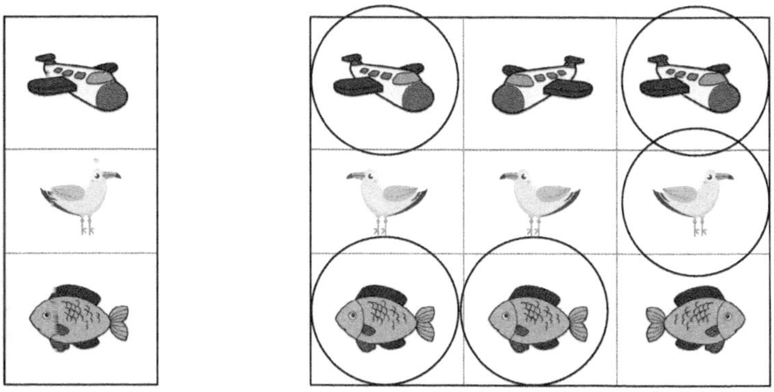

(f) Exercise 6: The mystery letter

- Ages: 7–8 years old
- Solution: The mystery letter is "A."

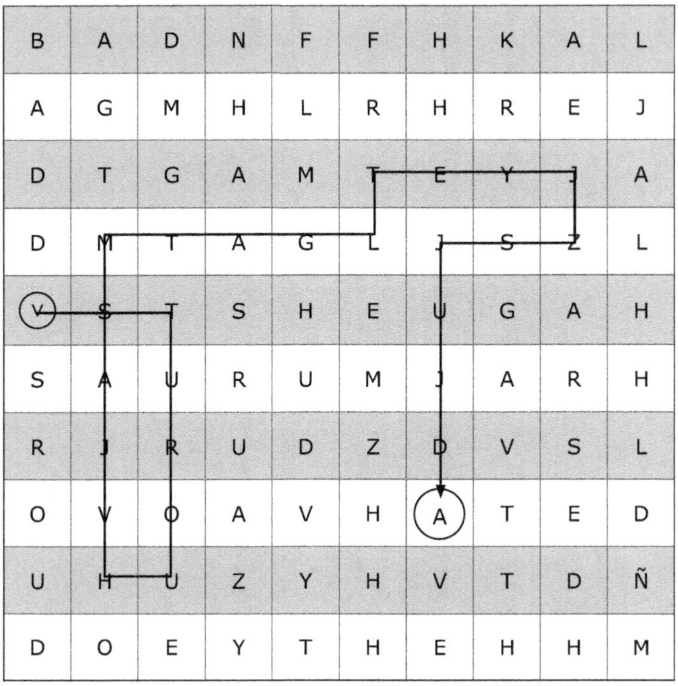

B	A	D	N	F	F	H	K	A	L
A	G	M	H	L	R	H	R	E	J
D	T	G	A	M	T	E	Y	J	A
D	M	T	A	G	L	J	S	Z	L
V	S	T	S	H	E	U	G	A	H
S	A	U	R	U	M	J	A	R	H
R	J	R	U	D	Z	D	V	S	L
O	V	O	A	V	H	A	T	E	D
U	H	U	Z	Y	H	V	T	D	Ñ
D	O	E	Y	T	H	E	H	H	M

(g) Exercise 7: Curves

- Ages: 6–7
- Solution:

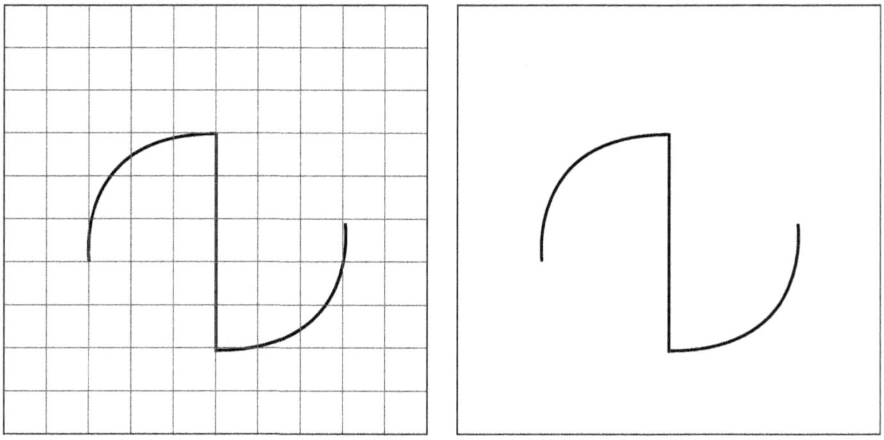

*(h) **Exercise 8: The other half***

- Ages: 7–8
- Solution:

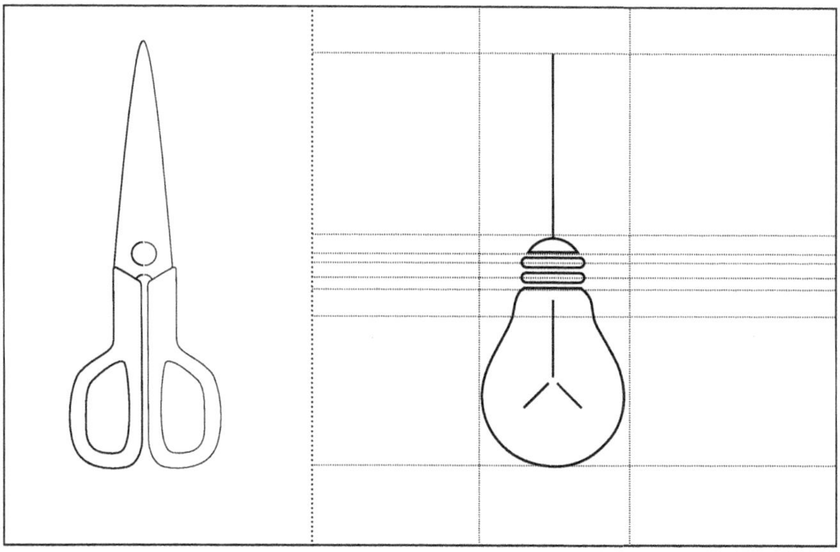

*(i) **Exercise 9: Making cubes***

- Ages: 7–8
- Solution:

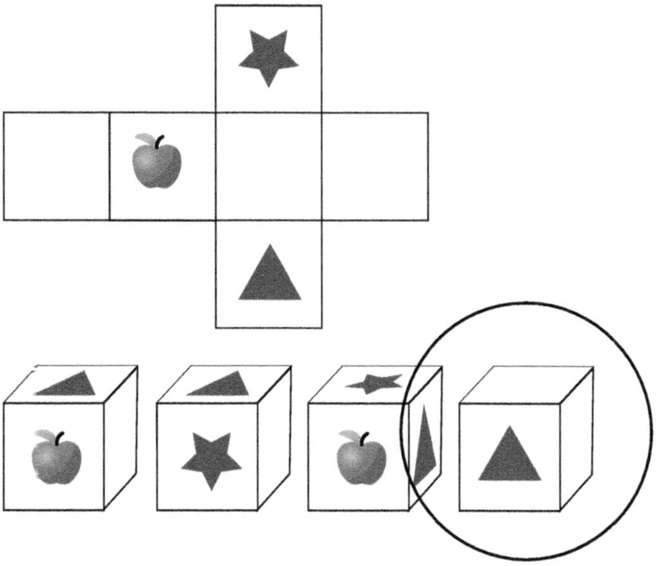

(j) Exercise 10: Rubén, Clara, and Rosa

- Ages: 5–6
- Solution:

What fruits are between Rubén and Clara? Apple, banana, and grapes.
Which fruit is farthest from Rosa? The apple.
What fruits are between Clara and Rosa? Peach and pear.
Which fruit is farthest from Clara? The pineapple.
Which fruit is farthest from Rubén? The pineapple.
Which sibling is closest to the grapes? Clara.
Which sibling is closest to the pineapple? Rosa.

(x) Chapter 16: The ten best board games for working on executive functions

(a) Exercise 1: Fast Flags®

- Ages: 8

(b) Exercise 2: The little clock

- Ages: 5–6 years and up

(c) Exercise 3: Speed Cups®

- Ages: 6 years and up

(d) Exercise 4: Cruel World®

- Ages: 8 years and up

(e) Exercise 5: Dobble®

- Ages: 6 and up, although there is a Dobble for younger children (4 years old)

(f) Exercise 6: Emotion!®

- Ages: 5–6 years and up

(g) Exercise 7: Cortex Challenge®

- Ages: 8 years and up

(h) Exercise 8: Touch and Find®

- Ages: 3 years and up

(i) Exercise 9: Ghost Blitz®

- Ages: 8–9 years and up

(j) Exercise 10: Mikado®

- Ages: 4 and up

Index

For Product Safety Concerns and Information please contact our EU representative GPSR@taylorandfrancis.com Taylor & Francis Verlag GmbH, Kaufingerstraße 24, 80331 München, Germany

Batch number: 10784123

Printed by Printforce, the Netherlands